Policy Failures in the Graveyard of Empires: How Policymakers Let the Soldiers Down in the British, the Soviet, and the American Wars in Afghanistan

Mehar Omar Khan

Policy Failures in the Graveyard of Empires

How Policymakers Let the Soldiers Down in the British, the Soviet, and the American Wars in Afghanistan

A Monograph
by
Maj Mehar Omar Khan
Pakistan Army

School of Advanced Military Studies
United States Army Command and General Staff College
Fort Leavenworth, Kansas

AY 2011

REPORT DOCUMENTATION PAGE

1. REPORT DATE *(DD-MM-YYYY)*	2. REPORT TYPE	3. DATES COVERED *(From - To)*
1 March 2011	SAMS Monograph	June 2010 – March 2011

4. TITLE AND SUBTITLE	
Policy Failures in the Graveyard of Empires: How policymakers let the soldiers down in the British, the Soviet, and the American wars in Afghanistan	5a. CONTRACT NUMBER
	5b. GRANT NUMBER
	5c. PROGRAM ELEMENT NUMBER

6. AUTHOR(S)	
Major Mehar Omar Khan (Pakistan Army)	5d. PROJECT NUMBER
	5e. TASK NUMBER
	5f. WORK UNIT NUMBER

7. PERFORMING ORGANIZATION NAME(S) AND ADDRESS(ES)	8. PERFORMING ORGANIZATION REPORT NUMBER
School of Advanced Military Studies (SAMS) 250 Gibbon Avenue Fort Leavenworth, KS 66027-2134	

9. SPONSORING / MONITORING AGENCY NAME(S) AND ADDRESS(ES)	10. SPONSOR/MONITOR'S ACRONYM(S)
Command and General Staff College 731 McClellan Avenue Fort Leavenworth, KS 66027-1350	CGSC
	11. SPONSOR/MONITOR'S REPORT NUMBER(S)

12. DISTRIBUTION / AVAILABILITY STATEMENT

Approved for Public Release; Distribution Unlimited

13. SUPPLEMENTARY NOTES

14. ABSTRACT

This monograph examines the role of policy in guidance of the British, the Soviet and the U.S.-NATO wars in Afghanistan. Set in the context of Afghanistan's history and its socio-cultural environment, the study critically analyzes the negative impact of policy failures - ac of both omission as well as commission - on the conduct and outcome of these three wars. Holding Afghanistan's physical environment as constant, the monograph examines numerous policy variables such as the evolution of grand strategy, resource allocation, governance, and security force assistance. A study of select aspects of the First Anglo-Afghan War and the Soviet Invasion of Afghanistan highlights sever policy missteps and miscalculations that, if heeded to, could have helped today's policymakers. The focus of the monograph, however, is on the ongoing U.S.-NATO effort. Based on some strikingly common and consistent errors of policy, the paper concludes that the incompetence and myopia of the policymakers is responsible for squandering the military gains and for failure to guide these wars to their strategic purpose and end state. In the end, the monograph puts forth a set of recommendations for both policymakers as well as operationa artists.

15. SUBJECT TERMS

The First Anglo-Afghan War, The Soviet Invasion, The U.S. NATO Campaign, Afghanistan, Policy Failures, Command and General Staf College, Operational Artists.

16. SECURITY CLASSIFICATION OF: (U)			17. LIMITATION OF ABSTRACT	18. NUMBER OF PAGES	19a. NAME OF RESPONSIBLE PERSOI Wayne W. Grigsby Jr. COL, U.S. Army
a. REPORT (U)	b. ABSTRACT (U)	c. THIS PAGE (U)	(U)	(U) 60	19b. TELEPHONE NUMBER *(include area code)* 913-364-4143

i

SCHOOL OF ADVANCED MILITARY STUDIES

MONOGRAPH APPROVAL

MAJ Mehar Omar Khan, Pakistan Army

Title of Monograph: Policy Failures in the Graveyard of Empires: How policymakers let the soldiers down in the British, the Soviet, and the American wars in Afghanistan

Approved by:

_____   Monograph Director
Daniel G. Cox, Ph. D

_____   Second Reader
Russell Livingston, COL, US Army

_____   Director,
Wayne W. Grigsby, Jr., COL, IN   School of Advanced
                                             Military Studies

_____   Director,
Robert F. Baumann, Ph.D.   Graduate Degree
                                             Programs

Abstract

POLICY FAILURES IN THE GRAVEYARD OF EMPIRES: HOW POLICYMAKERS LET THE
SOLDIERS DOWN IN THE BRITISH, THE SOVIET, AND THE AMERICAN WARS IN
AFGHANISTAN by Maj Mehar Omar Khan, Pakistan Army, 63 pages.

This monograph examines the role of policy in guidance of the British, the Soviet and the U.S.-
NATO wars in Afghanistan. Set in the context of Afghanistan's history and its socio-cultural
environment, the study critically analyzes the negative impact of policy failures - acts of both omission as
well as commission - on the conduct and outcome of these three wars. Holding Afghanistan's physical
environment as constant, the monograph examines numerous policy variables such as the evolution of
grand strategy, resource allocation, governance, and security force assistance. A study of select aspects of
the First Anglo-Afghan War and the Soviet Invasion of Afghanistan highlights several policy missteps
and miscalculations that, if heeded to, could have helped today's policymakers. The focus of the
monograph, however, is on the ongoing U.S.-NATO effort. Based on some strikingly common and
consistent errors of policy, the paper concludes that the incompetence and myopia of the policymakers is
responsible for squandering the military gains and for failure to guide these wars to their strategic purpose
and end state. In the end, the monograph puts forth a set of recommendations for both policymakers as
well as operational artists.

Table of Contents

INTRODUCTION

"These gentlemen (anti-Soviet Afghan *Mujahideen*) are the moral equivalents of America's founding fathers."

President Ronald Reagon, 1985[1]

Of all the places on earth, Afghanistan has historically been simultaneously the most prohibitive as well as the most alluring. It is prohibitive because of its widespread lawlessness, a treacherous terrain, and all the travails attached with travel through its length and breadth. Afghanistan is alluring to those who look for nature's beauty in its most rugged, raw, and pristine forms. It is attractive to those who can appreciate the "snow-peaks of the Hissar chain and the curtain of enchanting fields and spreading vineyards, which hides the hideous aspects of the Kara Kum."[2] Historically, however, this land of the feared tribesmen has ensnared foreigners less for *what* it is and more for *where* it is.

Afghanistan is also one place whose interaction with the outside world has brought scarce benefits to both. After hundreds of years of conflict, it is now a place where 165 out of every 1000 children die before reaching the age of one,[3] where an average human being does not expect to live longer than 45 years,[4] and where access to electricity is the lowest in the world.[5] If Afghanistan's present is so grim, its past has been no less sad. Succeeding generations of conquerors despoiled Afghanistan for reasons that had little to do with the country itself or even its people. Invariably, foreign powers, both from the region as well as the distant corners of the world, trampled Afghanistan as a gateway to the

---

[1] Akbar S. Ahmed, *Journey into America: The Challenge of Islam* (Washington, DC: Brookings Institution Press, 2010), 126.
[2] Angus Hamilton, *Afghanistan* (London: William Heinemann, 1906), 43-44.
[3] UNICEF, "Afghanistan," http://www.unicef.org/infobycountry/afghanistan_statistics.html (accessed September 20, 2010).
[4] CIA, "The World Fact Book," https://www.cia.gov/library/publications/the-world-factbook/geos/af.html (accessed September 20, 2010).
[5] The World Bank, "Afghanistan Country Overview," http://www.worldbank.org.af/WBSITE/EXTERNAL/COUNTRIES/SOUTHASIAEXT/AFGHANISTANEXTN/0,,contentMDK:20154015~menuPK:305992~pagePK:141137~piPK:141127~theSitePK:305985,00.html (accessed September 15, 2010).

irresistibly attractive Indus Plains or as a stepping stone to the Central Asian plateau. This place has thus become a poignant example of how geography can be an unshakable jinx.

A landlocked country, Afghanistan sits in the middle of the Central Asian steppes and the fertile plains on the banks of the mighty Indus, becoming what some call the "cross-roads of Central, West, and South Asia."[6] British historian Arnold Toynbee thought Afghanistan was the "roundabout of the world."[7] Owing mainly to its location, Cyrus of Persia (540 B.C.), Alexander the Great and his successors (circa 320-185 B.C.), Sassians (241-400 A.D.), Sassanians (642 A.D.) Arabs, and the Moguls of India,[8] all tried to control and rule Afghanistan with varying degrees of success but consistent levels of difficulty. While the foreigners came and went, the Afghan tribes continued to fight amongst themselves as well. Invasions and internal conflict have thus been a constant thread in Afghan history.

For over two thousand years, the Afghan region remained "deeply problematic for major empires from the West and the East – from the Arab armies to such legendary conquerors as Genghiz Khan, Timur (more commonly known as Tamerlane), and Babur."[9] Yet there are few takers for the lessons from history. The list of follies is not only long but also repetitive.

After colonizing the Indian Sub-Continent, the British rode headlong into repeated disasters in Afghanistan throughout the 19th and early 20th centuries. Russians were never far behind – under both the ambitious Czars as well as the expansionist Soviets. While the Czars were mostly content maintaining a comfortable degree of influence in Kabul, Communists chose to control and shape the Afghan state directly. What followed the Soviet occupation of Afghanistan is a story most Russians would love to forget. Soon after the Soviet departure in 1989, the US led coalition marched into Afghanistan with tens of thousands of men and a military wherewithal the world has rarely seen in its history. Powerless people

---

[6] Alfred Aghajanian, ed., *Afghanistan: Past and Present* (Los Angeles: IndoEuropean Publishing, 2007], 1.
[7] Peter Pigott, *Canada in Afghanistan: The War So Far* (Toronto: Dundurn Press, 2007), 18.
[8] Corey Gunderson, *Afghanistan's Struggles* (Edina, Minnesota: ABDO and Daughters, 2004], 15-17.
[9] Seth G. Jones, *In the Graveyard of Empires: America's War in Afghanistan* (New York: W.W. Norton and Company Inc., 2010), xxvi.

of lesser gods have watched as one great power after another takes turns pounding a vast expanse of barren hills and brave people.

Historians have struggled to explain why these great nations ventured into a campaign about which history's lessons were so terse and terrifying. Why would governments send their young men and women to die in vain? Why would the political leaders over-estimate the threat, over-dose the remedy, and under-resource the healing process? While all these questions are important, questioners often ignore another, deeper layer of fundamental questions. What was the wisdom, if any, of the very idea of *physically* invading Afghanistan? Moreover, having invaded, how have policies in Kabul affected the lives of fighting men in Kandahar and Kapisa? How has unwise employment of military forces and the fickle-minded mediocrity of the policymakers sabotaged military victories on the battlefield and in the end made the originally awe-inspiring militaries look feeble and incompetent?

This paper aspires to answer a question that has seldom gotten the space and seriousness it deserves. The paper contends that the recurring patterns of foreign failures in Afghanistan have little to do with the treacherous terrain or the ferocious tribesmen. Instead, it is the incompetence of the policymakers that repeatedly sabotaged military victories in hard-fought battles in the valleys and villages of Afghanistan. A study of the First Anglo-Afghan War, the Soviet Invasion and the NATO enterprise in Afghanistan supports this conclusion and will be used to show the veracity of the aforementioned thesis.

The British first got into Afghanistan in 1838. This war, called the First Anglo-Afghan War, lasted for over four years. The agonizingly clear part of the story of this war is that while the military accomplished its task of routing the existing regime and installing a puppet with spectacular speed and precision, the incompetence of the political captains of the ship turned the voyage into a nightmare. As the war protracted due to lack of a clear political guidance, a rising tide of insurgency forced British troops to try a number of tactics against the Afghans including the brutal "butcher and bolt."[10] In the military part of this war, there was no dearth of vile as well as valor, and yet they failed. The British

_____

[10] Jones, *In the Graveyard of Empires*, xxvi.

retreated in disgrace and only a few survived to tell the tale. Decades later, Churchill called the Afghans "a brave and warlike race."[11]

The analysis of the war has been both honest as well as revealing. J.A. Norris writes that "throughout the entire period of the British connection with Afghanistan, a strange moral *blindness* clouded the vision of the British statesmen wherein they saw only the natural, the inevitable results of their own measures, and forgot that those measures were the dragon's teeth from which sprung the armed men."[12] Captain Eric Sheppard of the Royal Tank Corps, writing in 1925, called it "one of the darkest chapters in the British history which has to tell not only of defeat but of disgrace, of shame as well as of sorrow."[13] While Sir John Fortscue called it "the insane enterprise," others condemned it as a "terrible mistake," "a blunder and a crime."[14] The chief architect of British policy towards Afghanistan has been "accused of straightforward wickedness," of being a "bumbling weakling without a settled policy of his own."[15] Though the British prestige was later in some measure repaired, the objects for which they took up arms were, in the ultimate outcome, left unattained.[16]

To be fair, the Soviets have not been nearly as honest about their debacle in Afghanistan in 1980s. After centuries of contest with the British over influence in Kabul and Tehran, the shame of physically invading and vandalizing Afghanistan came to the Communists under Leonid Brezhnev in 1979. Despite the fact that the Soviets had technically been 'invited' by the Afghan government, "they were widely perceived as foreign invaders."[17] The actual decision to invade was made in secret by a very small group of Politburo members, against the strong and openly expressed opposition of the military, and

---

[11] Sir Winston S. Churchill, *The Story of the Malakand Field Force* (London: Longman, Green, and Co., 1901), 274.
[12] J.A. Norris, *The First Afghan War 1838-1842* (Cambridge: University Press, 1967), xiv.
[13] Norris, *The First Afghan War,* xiv.
[14] Ibid., xv.
[15] Ibid.
[16] Ibid.
[17] Chris Johnson and Jolyol Leslie, *Afghanistan: The Mirage of Peace* (London: Zed Books Ltd, 2004), 142.

only then rubber-stamped by the other Politburo members.[18] In addition, Soviet leadership made the decision seemingly "on the basis of limited information."[19] Declassified Russian documents reveal, "Afghanistan did not fit into the mental maps and ideological constructs of the Soviet leaders."[20] The conceptual lens of Marxist-Leninist doctrine blinded the Soviet leadership to the realities of traditional tribal order of Afghanistan and led to the attempts to impose alien social and economic practices on the Afghan society, such as the forced land reform.[21]

In the end, Russia's own verdict about their misadventure in Afghanistan was the same: failure. On the eve of their departure from Kabul, Maj. Gen. Lev Serebrov, a political officer at the military headquarters in Kabul, told Western journalists: "We came here with an honorable task, with open hearts. We are leaving, and we have a sense of not having accomplished our mission to the end."[22] Decades after the war, the Soviet veterans talk about Afghanistan in terms that echo the American experience in Vietnam: "*of winning battles but losing the campaign,* watching the local population throw its support behind an insurgency and, finally, coming home to a country that no longer understood or supported their war."[23]

Almost two decades after the Soviet withdrawal, the US-led coalition seems to be bogged down in Afghanistan. On the eve of the 30th anniversary of the Soviet war, Tom Lasseter recounts how the somber and at times anguished way that veterans in Russia spoke of their time in Afghanistan was a disturbing reminder of the hurdles that American forces now face.[24] The initial successes of the US-

---

[18] Svetlana Savranskaya, ed., *"The Soviet Experience in Afghanistan: Russian Documents and Memoirs (The September 11th Sourcebooks, Volume-II), October 9, 2001,"* The National Security Archive, http://www.gwu.edu/~nsarchiv/NSAEBB/NSAEBB57/soviet.html (accessed September 20, 2010)
[19] Ibid.
[20] Ibid.
[21] Ibid.
[22] Soviet General Talks of Failure in Afghanistan, *The New York Times,* January 23, 1989, http://www.nytimes.com/1989/01/23/world/soviet-general-talks-of-failure-in-afghanistan.html (accessed September 23, 2010).
[23] Tom Lasseter, "Afghanistan war: Russian vets look back on their experience," *The Christian Science Monitor,* December 22, 2009, http://www.csmonitor.com/World/2009/1222/Afghanistan-war-Russian-vets-look-back-on-their-experience (accessed 23 Sep 2010).
[24] Ibid.

NATO mission seems to be losing relevance as uncertainty in policy clouds the mission and commitment of the soldiers on the ground. After initially aiming to just "smoke out and pursue evil doers, those barbaric people,"[25] the US political leadership expanded the mission into making Afghanistan "an American success story, a threshold democracy, and a model of what the Bush Administration's approach to nation-building can achieve." [26] A change in the administration in Washington, DC, brought with it another revision of the objectives. As the new President declared the United States would not aim to "rebuild Afghanistan into a Jeffersonian democracy,"[27] his Secretary of Defense thought a revision of goals was necessary because nobody in the world had that much time, patience or money.[28]

As the American War in Afghanistan ages to almost a decade, brave young soldiers and helpless, hopeless Afghans continue to die. While the belligerents on both sides continue to fight as hard as they did in 1840s and 1980s, the policy continues to falter in guiding the war to its end. This frightening scenario is what inspired this paper.

Structure and Method

To start with, a word on what this paper does not aim to be. It is not a comparative analysis of First Anglo-Afghan War, the Soviet Invasion, and the US-NATO Mission in Afghanistan. All these wars took place at radically different times, and in significantly different historical and geo-strategic contexts. The Anglo-Afghan War was first in a series of British expeditions to Afghanistan and even a disastrous defeat in this war, or the ones that succeeded it in late 19th and early 20th centuries, did not influence the British control of Indian sub-continent in any appreciable way. On the other hand, the Soviet Invasion and their ensuing retreat significantly contributed to the ultimate collapse of the Soviet empire in Central Asia. In the case of the US-NATO Mission, the jury is still out and the coalition still has a window, though

---

[25] Douglas Kellner, *From 9/11 to Terror War: The Dangers of the Bush Legacy* (Lanham, Maryland: Rowman & Littlefield Publishers, Inc., 2003), 58.

[26] Johnson and Leslie, *Afghanistan*, xii.

[27] Bobby Ghosh, "Afghan Mission Creep: Back to Nation-Building," *Time Magazine*, August 19, 2009, http://www.time.com/time/nation/article/0,8599,1917232,00.html#ixzz10NOf2tM9 (accessed September 23, 2010).

[28] Ibid.

increasingly narrow, of time to save face and arrange a relatively successful wrap-up of the war. This paper will also not recommend any definitive solutions. This is so because the insurgency in Afghanistan has always been a complex, terribly ill-structured problem that defies simple solutions.

Now, on to what this paper aims to do. In a nutshell, it is an attempt to use past analogies to help make sense of the present issues. It works with the assumption that "seeing the past can help one envision alternative futures."[29] While holding the physical environment of Afghanistan "constant," it will focus on political and strategic miscalculations and blunders that led to problems for the British, the Soviets and the US-NATO Missions in that country. The paper will attempt to indicate future paths by highlighting the past mistakes and will stop, as conceded above, short of recommending authoritative solutions. Due to a paucity of space, this paper will also not attempt to cover all aspects of "likeness and difference" between the analogies and their current parallel, as is done masterfully by Neustadt and May in their great work[30] examining the use of historical analogies for political decision-making. While there are significant differences amongst these three wars, this paper will attempt to highlight only the similarities in terms of policy formulation and implementation.

The research will follow a combination of deductive as well as inductive reasoning. In the interest of validity and fairness, the research draws on only the most consensual and widely known sources coming from almost all the countries involved. While use of history is of foundational importance for this work, contemporary analysis also figures prominently.

The opening section is an attempt to arrange Afghanistan's past as a foundation for understanding its present. It will focus on historical milestones, events, and salient trends that have shaped Afghan polity and the social and religious outlook of its people. This section will also deal with some oft-repeated questions about Afghan demography and the famed ferocity of the Afghan fighters. It will explore issues

---

[29] Richard E. Neustadt and Earnest R. May, *Thinking in Time: The Uses of History for Decision Makers* (New York: The Free Press, 1988), xv.
[30] Ibid., 37-42.

such as Afghanistan's evolution and survival as a state without being a nation, and the explosive mix of religion and tribal tradition.

The second section briefly covers the importance of understanding the role of geography in Afghanistan. The purpose is to set a stage for easier understanding of a complex confluence of geo-strategic factors that have affected the causes, the course, and the outcomes of historical events in Afghanistan. This section explores why the internal geography of Afghanistan, contrary to the popular perception and analysis, has not been a (or the) *decisive* factor in the history of unsuccessful attempts to control this country.

The paper arrives at its purpose in its third section. Here, it will, with insights from the British, the Soviet and the US-NATO experiences in Afghanistan, lay out how politics of occupation have been responsible for the repeated mess in Afghanistan. Presenting a concise analysis of myriad policy blunders, this section will get most of the space and energy of this paper. It will address such issues as the grand strategy, initial intent, mission creep, resource allocation, and lack of appreciation for local culture and tradition. It will also attempt to find answers to some of the most enduring questions about the clash of value systems, the conflict of precedence between life and liberty, tribe and state, proximate fears and the long-term future.

An epilogue will proffer some recommendations and suggestions for the policymakers as well the operational artists. These recommendations are not intended to be solutions to the current problems. Instead, they point to the general direction in which the policymakers and operational planners must look when seeking solutions.

SECTION-I

A Brief History of Conquest, Conflict, and Courage

"If you look at the past, we don't think it strange that America will attack us. Unfortunately, it is our fate that everyone attacks us."

Mullah Wakil Ahmed Mutawakkil in 1999[31]

Landmarks, Trials, and Tragedies

George Santayana's observation that "those who cannot remember the past are condemned to repeat it" applies to Iraq, but even more so to Afghanistan and western Pakistan's Federally Administered Tribal Areas [FATA].[32] It is almost impossible to understand the present state of this region without a peek into Afghanistan's history. What follows therefore is a quick look through the salient stories of Afghan history before arriving at some of the most prominent and consistent trends this history indicates. These trends will hopefully establish why some policies have not been successful in Afghanistan.

Afghanistan served as the gateway to India, especially for the invaders from central and western Asia. In 328 B.C.E., Alexander the Great entered the territory of present-day Afghanistan to capture Bactria (present-day Balkh). Invasions by the Scythians, White Huns, and the Turks followed in succeeding centuries. In 642 B.C.E., Arabs invaded the entire region and introduced Islam.[33] Arab rule quickly gave way to the neighboring Persians, who controlled the area until the Turkic Ghaznavids' conquest in 998.

Mahmud of Ghazni (998-1030) consolidated the conquests of his predecessors and turned Ghazni, located southwest of Kabul, into a great cultural center as well as a base for frequent forays into India. Between 1001 and his death in 1030 C.E., Mahmud launched seventeen raids on India. Following Mahmud's short-lived dynasty, various princes attempted to rule sections of the region until the Mongol invasion of 1219.

---

[31]Michael Griffin, *Reaping the Whirlwind: The Taliban Movement in Afghanistan* (Sterling, VA: Pluto Press, 2001), 211.

[32] Volney F.Warner, "Context and What's Next," *Joint Forces Quarterly 56* (1st quarter, 2010): 19.

[33] Country Watch, *Afghanistan: 2010 Country Review* (Houston, Texas: CountryWatch, Inc., 2010), 7.

The Mongols, led by Genghis Khan, plundered Afghanistan's fertile agricultural areas and destroyed several bustling cities including Herat, Ghazni, and Balkh. Many historians believe that the Mongol barbarities were one of the main reasons that sent the region into decline.[34] After Genghis Khan's brutal raids, "much of the remaining population reverted to nomadism."[35] Following Genghis Khan's death, Tamerlane incorporated Afghanistan into his vast empire. Babur, a descendant of Tamerlane and the founder of India's Mogul Dynasty at the beginning of the 16th century, made Kabul the capital of an Afghan principality.

After the decline of the Turko-Mongol dynasties in the 18th century, a grouping of several *Pashtun* tribes founded their own empire.[36] In 1747, Ahmad Shah Durrani (a *Pashtun* and an ancestor of both Mullah Omar and Hamid Karzai) defeated Moguls and took charge in Delhi. Most Afghans consider him the founder of the modern day Afghanistan. Throughout his reign, Durrani consolidated chieftainships, petty principalities, and fragmented provinces into one country. All of Afghanistan's rulers, until the 1978 Marxist coup d'etat, proudly trace their roots to Durrani's *Pashtun* tribal confederation, and *all* have been members of the tribe's Mohammadzai clan after 1818. It was under Durrani's that "*Pashtun* tribes finally emerged as the dominant ethnic group in Afghanistan."[37]

After India's colonization by the British during the 19th century, Afghanistan found itself sandwiched between the expanding British and the Russian empires. British concern over Russian advances in Central Asia and growing influence in Persia culminated in the two Anglo-Afghan Wars. The first (1838-42) resulted not only in the destruction of a British army, but is remembered today as an example of the ferocity of Afghan resistance to foreign rule. This tug-of-war between Russia and British India left a seminal mark on Afghanistan's evolution as a state. Barnett Rubin believes, "Afghanistan confronted modernity through its forced integration into the Eurocentric state system as a buffer between

---

[34] Barnett R. Rubin, *The Fragmentation of Afghanistan* (Yale University Press, 2002), 19.
[35] Ibid., 22.
[36] Ibid., 19.
[37] Goodson, *Afghanistan's Endless War*, 29.

the Russian and the British empires." [38] He further asserts that the formation and transformation of that state system created the contending forces of the conflict at play in and around Afghanistan to this day. [39]

As the sun was setting on the British empire in India, Muhammad Zahir Shah ascended to the throne in Kabul in 1933. He ruled Afghanistan until 1973. Zahir Shah made some brave but abortive attempts to catapult a medieval society into a modern state. In 1964, he promulgated a liberal constitution allowing the growth of political parties including the communist People's Democratic Party of Afghanistan (PDPA), which later broke into two rival factions: the Khalq (Masses) and the Parcham (Banner) faction. Zahir Shah's attempts to bring about for his country, what Barnett Rubin calls a "forced integration into the contemporary state system," [40] resulted in further fragmentation of the society and strengthening of traditionalism and localism.

Zahir's rule ended abruptly when his cousin, Sardar Mohammad Daoud, seized power in a military coup on July 17, 1973. Daoud abolished the monarchy, abrogated the 1964 constitution, and declared Afghanistan a republic with himself as its first president as well as prime minister. Seeking to exploit the mounting disaffection of the populace, the PDPA reunified with Moscow's support. [41] On April 27-28, 1978, the PDPA initiated a bloody coup that resulted in the overthrow and death of Daoud and most of his family. Nur Muhammad Taraki, Secretary General of the PDPA, became president of the Revolutionary Council and prime minister of the newly established 'Democratic' Republic of Afghanistan.

During first 18 months of its rule, PDPA brutally imposed a Marxist-style "reform" program, which ran counter to the deeply rooted Islamic tradition. By the summer of 1978, a major revolt in the Nuristan region of eastern Afghanistan spread into a countrywide insurgency. In September 1979, Hafizullah Amin seized power from Taraki after a palace shootout. Over the next two months, instability

---

[38] Rubin, *The Fragmentation of Afghanistan*, 5.
[39] Ibid.
[40] Rubin, *The Fragmentation of Afghanistan*, 15.
[41] Country Watch, *Afghanistan: 2010 Country Review*, 10.

plagued Amin's regime as he moved against perceived enemies within the PDPA. By December, party morale was crumbling, and the insurgency was growing. The Soviet Union moved quickly to take advantage of the situation and signed a new bilateral treaty of 'friendship and cooperation' with Afghanistan.

The survival of the PDPA regime became increasingly dependent upon Soviet military equipment and advisers, and over time, the Afghan army began to collapse. By October 1979, however, relations between Afghanistan and the Soviet Union soured as Amin turned down Soviet advice on how to stabilize and consolidate his government. On December 24, 1979, large numbers of Soviet airborne forces, joining thousands of Soviet troops already on the ground, began to land in Kabul under the pretext of a field exercise but actually to teach Amin a lesson. Two days later, the invasion forces killed Hafizullah Amin and installed Babrak Karmal, an exiled leader of the Parcham faction, as the prime minister. Massive Soviet ground forces invaded from the north on December 27.

An overwhelming majority of Afghans opposed the puppet communist regime, either actively or passively. Afghan *mujahedeen* (freedom fighters) made it almost impossible for the regime to maintain a system of local government outside major urban centers. Poorly armed at first, in 1984 the *mujahedeen* began receiving substantial assistance in the form of weapons and training from the United States and other outside powers. During the 1980s, due to the efforts of people like Rep. Charlie Wilson, the United States steered "billions of dollars in secret funding to the C.I.A. to funnel arms to the *mujahedeen*."[42] In May 1985, the US-backed Peshawar-based guerrilla organizations formed an alliance to coordinate their political and military operations against the Soviet occupation. Late in 1985, the *mujahedeen* were active in and around Kabul, launching rocket attacks and assassinating high government officials. The failure of the Soviet Union to win over a significant number of Afghan collaborators, or to rebuild a viable

---

[42] David Johnston, "Charlie Wilson's War: Arming the Mujahedeen," *New York Times,* May 25, 2003, http://www.grailwerk.com/docs/nytimes10.htm (accessed on October 5, 2010).

Afghan army, forced it to bear an increasing responsibility for fighting the resistance and for running the government.

Only after more than 41% Afghan children between the age of 8 and 18 had "lost one or both parents,"[43] 13,310 Russian soldiers had been killed and another 35,478 wounded,[44] did Moscow decide to withdraw in 1989. Their puppet in Kabul, Najibullah, lasted only three more years. As soon as the villainous Uzbek warlord Abdul Rashid Dostum, a criminal who would once again rise to prominence and prestige under US-sponsored post-*Taliban* Karzai regime, defected in March 1992, Najibullah regime collapsed. With the demise of their common enemy, the militias' ethnic, clan, religious, and personality differences re-surfaced, and the civil war raged on unabated. Najibullah himself, hiding for years in a UN compound in Kabul, was shot dead along with his brother on 26 September 1996, and their bodies were then strung up on a pole outside the presidential palace.[45]

As the Soviets were leaving Afghanistan, former freedom fighters turned on each other with a vengeance rarely seen in human quarrels. Consequently, "Afghanistan changed from the West's valiant ally waging a frontline war against communist expansion, into a rogue state, home to drug traffickers, Islamist terrorists, and bloody warlords."[46] In late 1994, a force called the *Taliban* (generic interpretation: students, literal meaning: seekers), consisting of primarily *Pashtun* refugees,[47] took Afghanistan by storm, vowing to install an Islamic government. The group systematically pushed aside most other factions and

---

[43] Leila Gupta, *Psychosocial Assessment of Children Exposed to War Related Violence in Kabul* (New York: UNICEF, 1997)

[44] Philip Taubman, "Soviet Lists Afghan War Toll: 13,310 Dead, 35,478 Wounded," *New York Times*, May 26, 1988, http://www.nytimes.com/1988/05/26/world/soviet-lists-afghan-war-toll-13310-dead-35478-wounded.html (accessed October 5, 2010).

[45] William Reeves, "Obituary: Dr Najibullah," *The Independent* (UK), September 28, 1996, http://www.independent.co.uk/news/obituaries/obituary-dr-najibullah-1365378.html (accessed on October 5, 2010).

[46] Goodson, *Afghanistan's Endless War*, ix.

[47] CNN, "Who are the Taliban of Afghanistan," October 05, 1996, http://articles.cnn.com/1996-10-05/world/9610_05_taleban_1_taliban-islamic-militia-kabul-islamic-afghanistan?_s=PM:WORLD (accessed on October 5, 2010).

gradually took control of several provinces. Although initially many Afghans welcomed the Taliban, opinions changed as the movement fought to "extend its harsh rule over the entire nation."[48]

After the 9/11 barbarities in the United States in 2001, the Taliban "refused to turn over suspected terrorist mastermind Osama bin Laden and disregarded the American threat to its regime."[49] The United States struck in the first week of October 2001. The Taliban retreated into their mountain hideouts and a new regime under Hamid Karzai came to power in Kabul. Almost a decade and thousands of deaths later, *Pashtuns* under a Durrani by the name of Omar (better known as Mullah Omar) continue to fight for a return to Kabul as the US-NATO coalition fights on in support of its preferred rulers in Kabul.

Common and Consistent Trends in Afghan History

Modern Afghan citizens are a product of myriad cruel interactions between history, geography, religion, and tradition. It is hard for an outsider to gain a grasp of Afghan attitudes without looking, primarily, at their history of interaction with the foreigners. The ensuing paragraphs highlight some of the salient historical trends that have shaped Afghan behavior, customs, and attitudes.

Afghans have for centuries "lived off the duties levied on long distance traders who crossed their land by such routes as the famous Silk Road."[50] In the latter half of the 19th century, Amir Abdur Rahman Khan (1881-1901) dreamt of establishing a modern Afghan state but soon realized that "without steady foreign aid, he could not implement his plan to transform Afghanistan into a modern autocracy."[51] After he accepted the British suzerainty, the British India lavished weapons and cash on a pliable Amir Abdur Rahman Khan regime and his successors. After the departure of the British from India, the Soviet Union took over the dubious role of Afghanistan's suzerain and sustainer. For decades thereafter, Kabul witnessed a succession of *Pashtun* rulers "using external resources to reign over an ethnically

---

[48] Christiane Amanpour, "Tyranny of the Taliban," *Time Magazine*, June 24, 2001, http://www.time.com/time/magazine/article/0,9171,1101971013-136677,00.html (accessed October 5, 2010).
[49] Michael A. Lev, "Taliban maintains refusal to turn over bin Laden," *Los Angeles Times*, October 3, 2001, http://www.latimes.com/sns-worldtrade-taliban-chi,0,1586746.story (accessed on October 5, 2010).
[50] Rubin, *The Fragmentation of Afghanistan*, 19.
[51] Ibid., 19-20.

heterogeneous society while manipulating that social segmentation to weaken the society's resistance."[52] The pattern continues to this day and the actual rulers of this country still come from places outside of Afghanistan. This explains the seemingly unbridgeable gap between the rebellious man of the mountain and the king's men in Kabul.

Despite the servile attitude of the ruling elite in Kabul, tribes' fights against invaders and amongst themselves have led to a society that is, in David Isby's words, "framed for resistance but very hard to organize."[53] The tribesmen's tendency to look askance at control in the name of unity comes from a long history of betrayals and treachery. As Volney Warner notes, "These people have little desire for social or economic intercourse with strangers because history has convinced them that such interchanges only benefit the stranger."[54] Moreover, "despite its location, and perhaps because of it, Afghanistan's people have exhibited fierce independence and martial skill throughout recorded history, making neither their military performance against the Soviet Union in the 1980s nor their continued civil war especially remarkable."[55] Larry Goodson believes that, for an Afghan, underlying all else is the desire for independent decision-making exhibited repeatedly throughout their history.[56]

Afghans' rules for recognition of a ruler as legitimate are unique. Afghan history demonstrates conclusively that "legitimacy of governance comes exclusively from two immutable sources: *dynastic* (monarchies and tribal patriarchies) and *religious*, or sometimes both."[57] This applies not just to Kabul but every valley and village across Afghanistan. The resistance to reform of this tradition is especially intense in *Pashtun* hills and hamlets, "where dynastic and religious authority has been unquestioned for over a thousand years."[58]

---

[52] Rubin, *The Fragmentation of Afghanistan*, 19.
[53] David C. Isby, *War in a Distant Country: Afghanistan Invasion and Resistance* (London: Arms and Armour Pess, 1989), 12.
[54] Warner, "Context and What's Next," 19.
[55] Goodson, *Afghanistan's Endless War*, 23.
[56] Ibid., 24.
[57] Thomas Barfield, "Problems of Establishing Legitimacy in Afghanistan," *Iranian Studies* 37 (2004): 263-269.
[58] Thomas H. Johnson and M. Chris Mason, "Refighting the Last War: Afghanistan and the Vietnam Template," *Military Review* (November-December 2009): 5.

Over the last few centuries, Afghans have evolved a "unity of values often cited by *Pashtuns* as a motivation for participating in Jihad: for Islam, for homeland and for honor. *(da islam da para, da watan da para, da namus da para)*."[59] In the midst of a mutual fight, an invasion could weld them together in a common cause.[60] Reinforcing their warlike nature is the *Pashtun* tribal code known as the *Pashtunwali*. Although *Pashtunwali* is a conglomerate of local tribal codes, certain primary themes include "*melmastia* and *mehrmapalineh* (both concerning hospitality to guests), *nanawati* (the right of asylum), *badal* (the right of revenge), *tureh* (bravery), *meranah* (manhood), *isteqamat* (persistence), *sabat* (steadfastness), *imandari* (righteousness), *ghayrat* (defense of property and honor) and *namus* (defense of the honor of women)."[61] This tradition explains why, in response to American demand to hand over Osama bin Laden, Mullah Omar declared that to agree to the American request would be "a betrayal and a breach of the Afghan tradition of hospitality."[62]

The turbulent history has also turned Afghans into, in the words of David Isby, "fighting men who are tough, committed, implacable, and tremendously brave." [63] Larry Goodson believes that the tribesmen's continued martial capability in the face of significant changes in military tactics and weapons has "ensured the survival of Afghanistan."[64] During their forays through Central Asian steppes and the plains of Punjab, all the great conquerors were "bedeviled by the ferocious tenacity of the indigenous hill tribes and steppe nomads who engaged them."[65] For centuries now, these men of the mountain have represented to the West, what Barnett Rubin believes has been "the firmest resistance to its power and domination." [66] Kipling's ballad of the encounter between a *Pashtun* tribesman and a Scottish soldier of the British imperial army shows his admiration for the Afghans' fighting skills:

---

[59] Rubin, *The Fragmentation of Afghanistan*, xvii.
[60] Goodson, *Aghanistan's Endless War*, 24.
[61] Ibid., 16.
[62] Jason Burke, "Bin Laden ready to leave hideout," *Guardian UK*, October 31, 1999, http://www.guardian.co.uk/world/1999/oct/31/afghanistan (accessed September 16, 2010).
[63] Isby, *War in a Distant Country,* 12.
[64] Goodson, *Afghanistan's Endless War*, 36.
[65] Ibid., 23.
[66] Rubin, *The Fragmentation of Afghanistan*, 3.

Oh, East is East, and West is West and never the twain shall meet,
Till Earth and Sky stand presently at God's great Judgment Seat,
But there is neither East nor West, border, nor breed, nor birth,
When two strong men stand face to face, though they come from the ends of the earth![67]

However, in his attitude towards women, the chivalrous Afghan fighter has a not-so-heroic side

as well. This critical aspect of Afghan society, sad though it is, needs understanding more than

unqualified condemnation. Male domination and chauvinism are perhaps the most prominent societal side

effects of ceaseless warfare and women's dependence on their men during this state to near constant

violence. However, male chauvinism in Afghan society is not a recent nor transient phenomenon that can

be corrected by shaming Afghans through antics like a picture of an Afghan girl with her nose chopped

off allegedly by Taliban insurgents on the cover of Time Magazine.[68] The problem is deeper than that

and, thus, so must be the solution. Unfortunately, "sex roles and attitude toward women in Afghanistan

are reflected in the language and literature, religion, educational system, employment and the family."[69]

A fuller understanding of the gender biases in Afghanistan can best come from the history of the

country. The tragically recurring need for Afghan men to fight and often die in large numbers for their

land and honor has somewhat legitimated their special status within the family. Resultantly, men's

privileged status is about as much granted by women as it is demanded and wrested by men themselves.

Particularly amongst *Pashtuns*, another element of women's self-image comes from "the belief that men,

for all their posturing, are weaker than women, and that women could defend *namus* at least as well if

they had the chance - and the guns."[70] History bears testimony to the latter claim. Here is how Kipling

portrays the ferocity of the Afghan woman:

When you're wounded and left on Afghanistan's plains,
And the women come out to cut up what remains,

---

[67] Rudyard Kipling, *The Writings in Prose and Verse of Rudyard Kipling* (New York: Charles Scribner's Sons, 1899), 61. Google e-book.
[68] Aryn Baker, "Afghan Women and the Return of the Taliban," *Time*, July 29, 2010, http://www.time.com/time/world/article/0,8599,2007238,00.html#ixzz0xXWOtjMb (accessed August 24, 2010).
[69] Ehsan M. Entezar, *Afhanistan 101: Understanding Afghan Culture* (USA: Xlibris Corporation, 2007), 146.
[70] Rubin, *The Fragmentation of Afghanistan*, 41.

Jest roll to your rifles and blow out your brains,
An' go to your Gawd like a soldier.[71]

The spirit of the Afghan woman also glows through the legend of Malalai who prevented Afghan retreat at Maiwand in 1880 by holding her veil aloft as a banner and shouting the famous Pashtu couplet:

My beloved, if you do not fall a martyr in battle at Maiwand,
By God, someone must be saving you for a life of shame.[72]

Warfare breeds and thrives on distrust. Distrust in turn manifests itself in distance between man and man and amidst a people in general. A society that goes through perpetual warfare turns into a *lashkar* (one large militia) where relationships are all hierarchical. Afghanistan is one such high power-distance society where a father is a distant authority for son, a husband as remote as stars for his wife, and a chief of the tribe an inaccessible, unquestionable authority for the common folk. It is a society where "who you know (*rawabit*, connections) rather than what you know (*zawabit*, principles) is what counts."[73] Unlike western countries, older people do not allow younger people to take decision-making in their hands. For the same reason, Afghans do not trust leaders younger than fifty years of age.[74] Resultantly, despite several attempts at reform and modernization, the patriarchal family has been "the most successfully enforced form of social control, as well as the basic institution of consumption and production."[75]

Contrary to the popular perception, in Afghanistan, tradition is arguably as important as the word of God. It is normal to bend the religious guidance here and there in the service of the tradition. Despite the fact that the Afghan state has dabbled in "radical political ideologies from Communism to Islamism,"[76] tribal codes continue to occupy the central place in Afghan society. Larry Goodson observes

---

[71] Joseph Rudyard Kipling, *The Works of Rudyard Kipling* (The Forgotton Books, 2008), 109.
[72] Rubin, *The Fragmentation of Afghanistan*, 25.
[73] Entezar, *Afhanistan 101*, 141.
[74] Ibid., 143.
[75] Rubin, *The Fragmentation of Afghanistan*, 41.
[76] Ibid.

that "Afghanistan's religious framework is based on a syncratic blend of various interpretations of Islamic doctrine with local customs, making the country simultaneously unified by one faith and divided by hundreds of variations on its practice."[77] Perhaps this explains why, despite the fact that leading religious families are respected and venerated, Afghans have "never been governed by religious leaders."[78]

With respect to ceaseless infighting, David Isby compares Afghan tribes to other mountain peoples such as Scots highlanders and American Appalachians who have also experienced inter-tribal and inter-group feuding.[79] For centuries, the Afghan region was a grey area in which petty warlords rose and fell, quarreled with each other, and sometimes allied themselves with Persian or other invaders, switching loyalties whenever it was expedient.[80] Afghanistan's population suffers from deep and multifaceted cleavages. Religious, sectarian, tribal, and racial divisions feed into ethnic and linguistic differences. Additionally, all these divisions, according to Larry Goodson, "are reinforced by spatial pattern of population distribution into different regions of the country."[81] However, despite all the inter-tribe bloodshed, Afghanistan has rarely witnessed a significant internal threat or challenge to its continued existence as a unified country. Afghanistan's history of foreign invasions seems to be one of the main reasons for this paradox. David Isby supports this assumption and believes that "being at the crossroads of Asia and diversity of race and culture may have contributed to the degree of toleration that has traditionally existed in Afghanistan."[82]

For the Afghans, the mountains represent honor and the life of cities supposedly inhibits the pristine spirit of unbridled freedom. This perspective seems to be behind the origin of *Pashto* saying: Honor ate up the mountains; taxes ate up the plains. The difference between the *nang* (honor associated with mountain) and *qalang* (taxes associated with city life on the plains) tribes is central to *Pashtun* self-

---

[77] Goodson, *Afghanistan's Endless War*, 12.
[78] J. Bruce Amstutz, *Afghanistan: The First Five Years of Soviet Occupation* (Washington DC: National Defense University Press, 1986), 125.
[79] Isby, *War in a Distant Country,* 12.
[80] Edgar O'Ballance, *Afghan Wars: Battles in a Hostile Land* (UK: Brassey's, 2002), 3.
[81] Goodson, *Afghanistan's Endless War*, 12.
[82] Isby, *War in a Distant Country*, 11.

image. According to Barnett Rubin, "The *Qalang Pashtuns* collect taxes and represent the state, while the *Nang* are considered the true embodiment of *Pashtunwali* (the honor code of *badal* (vengeance), *melmastia* (hospitality) and *nanawati* (asylum to the fugitive))." [83] The spirit of freedom amongst the mountain tribes has survived unmolested because as the invaders ravaged the cities, the mountain people managed to "hide out until the tides of death and destruction had rolled past them."[84]

Summing up, the Afghan history indicates several prominent trends that can serve as invaluable guides to understanding this country and its people. Firstly, because of the *nang–qalang* divide, control of the cities does not necessarily translate into a control of the mountains. Secondly, a legitimate ruler will have to combine in him a high religious standing as well as notable tribal lineage. Thirdly, traditionally an Afghan has never been too happy to subordinate his tradition to his religion. Fourthly, issues such as human rights, women rights, and civic freedoms have a peculiar connotation for Afghan society. Lastly, ground realities like a high power-distance must be allowed to moderate ideals like universal franchise and Westminster democracy.

---

[83] Rubin, *The Fragmentation of Afghanistan*, 28.
[84] O'Ballance, *Afghan Wars*, 2.

SECTION-II

The Myth of Geography

"In Afghanistan, a small army would be annihilated and a large one starved"

Arthur Wellesley, Duke of Wellington[85]

Most historians believe modern Afghanistan is result of a "confluence of geography and demography."[86] While conceding that Afghanistan owes its continued, though painful, existence as an independent state to the fighting spirit of its people, historians ascribe even the guerilla expertise to the extremely rugged terrain of Afghanistan and the tribal areas of North West Frontier Province of Pakistan.[87] The author of this paper however considers that most accounts have generally over-stated the importance of terrain. Without reproducing cumbersome details about the lay of the Afghan land, this section will attempt to prove how and why, contrary to the popular perception, the so-called treacherous terrain is not *responsible* for the defeat of foreign missions in Afghanistan.

Mountainous terrain, especially in the eastern Afghanistan, has seldom been a *decisive* factor in the outcome of battles because of two main reasons: firstly, most of the invaders lost their most decisive battles in and around the cities and not in the hills or passes in the countryside, and, secondly, the battles fought in the Uzbek and Tajik areas to the north and northwest of the country were as fierce and seminal as those in the east and southeast. It is also important to reiterate that foreign forces won most of the battles and still their nations lost the war. What follows is an expansion of these two arguments.

The Meeting Grounds

The British fought[88] and comprehensively won their main battles in and around some of the major towns in central Afghanistan. In July 1839, the British-Indian Army along with the army of Shah Shuja thrashed the Afghan resistance fighters in the Battle of Ghazni in Central Afghanistan. It was again in

---

[85] David Loyn, *In Afghanistan: Two Hundred Years of British, Russian and American Occupation* (New York: Pelgrave MacMillan, 2009), 11.
[86] Goodson, *Afghanistan's Endless War*, 23.
[87] Ibid., 37.
[88] First Afghan War, http://britishbattles.com/first-afghan-war/kabul-1842.htm (accessed September 23, 2010)

Central Afghanistan where, in Battle of Kabul and the retreat to Gandamak circa January 1842, the British imperial forces trounced the Ghilzai tribesmen. In April 1842, the British Indian Army and the soldiers of Shah Shuja completed a successful siege of Jalalabad. Again, in 1842, the British forces, garrisoned in the heart of the city, successfully defended Kabul against a massive onslaught of Afghan levies and tribesmen.

The Soviets fought most of their decisive engagements in and around major cities. They also faced some stiff resistance from areas other than and different from the Pashtun heartland to the east and the south. Between 1980 and 1985, the Russians launched as many as nine offensives into the strategically important Panjshir Valley,[89] a place far away and different from the treacherous mountains of the Pakistan-Afghanistan Border. Heavy fighting also occurred in the provinces neighboring Pakistan, where "cities and government outposts (*not the passes and gorges*) were constantly under siege by the *mujahideen*."[90] The cities of Herat and Kandahar remained hotbeds of resistance and were always partly controlled by the resistance.[91]

The US-NATO military operations against resistance fighters have generally met spectacular successes in isolated engagements in the mountains. The notorious passes and gorges have posed minimal problems as, barring occasional and relatively recent diplomatic spats with Pakistan,[92] the Coalition's supplies have flowed fairly smoothly along the lines of communications running through areas where tribesmen inflicted the most horrendous losses on the British (1840s) and the Soviets (1980s). However, the most serious challenges to the Coalition-Kabul government have come from cities and towns like

---

[89] Lester W. Grau and Michael A. Gress, *The Soviet Afghan War: How a Super Power Fought and Lost / The Russian General Staff* (Lawrence: University Press of Kansas, 2002), 26.
[90] Mohammad Yousaf and Mark Adkin, *Afghanistan The Bear Trap: The Defeat of a Superpower* (Casemate, 1992), 159.
[91] Olivier Roy, *Islam and Resistance in Afghanistan* (Cambridge University Press, 1990), 191.
[92] Declan Walsh, "Pakistan blocks Nato supply route to Afghanistan," *Guardian UK*, September 30, 2010, http://www.guardian.co.uk/world/2010/sep/30/pakistan-blocks-nato-route-afghanistan (accessed October 14, 2010).

Kandahar and Marjah. A recent coalition assault on Marjah was not entirely successful[93] and Kandahar continues to be a hotbed of Taliban activity.[94]

Therefore, while the craggy mountains of Afghanistan may inspire awe, the challenge has traditionally resided in the population centers. The guerillas may have traditionally thrived in the mountains, they have invariably chosen cities and population centers for their decisive blows. Even today, the wilderness of Helmand province in southern Afghanistan is considered the "ground-zero for the Taliban insurgency."[95] Stanley McChrystal, former top US General in Afghanistan, identified the control of, inter alia, Kandahar City and the surrounding areas as key to success in Afghanistan.[96]

History of Resistance in Western Afghanistan

The second important historical reality that contradicts the popular myth about the decisive role of eastern mountains, relates to the significant contribution of non-*Pashtun* people to their nation's wars against foreign interventions and occupations. The story of Afghanistan's freedom struggle is incomplete without the heroics of Tajiks from the west, Hazaras from the center, and Uzbeks from the northwest of the country. In this regard, places like Herat, Mazar-i-Sharif, Kunduz, and Panjshir stand out as prominently as Kandahar, Jalabad, Ghazni, and Gardez in the east.

The British campaign in 1838 ousted a *Pashtun* ruler from Kabul and installed another *Pashtun* in his place. Most of the action and counteraction therefore centered on *Pashtun* tribes and their hinterland along what is now the Pakistan-Afghanistan border. However, the role of Uzbek, Tajik and Hazara tribes - most of whom live in the central, northern and western parts of Afghanistan – was no less significant in the resistance against the British control of Kabul. Historical records reveal that after Shah Shuja

---

[93] Abigail Hauslohner, "As McChrystal Stumbles, the U.S. Campaign in Marjah Struggles," *Time Magazine*, June 22, 2010, http://www.time.com/time/world/article/0,8599,1998620,00.html (accessed October 14, 2010).
[94] Joshua Partlow, "In Kandahar, the Taliban targets and assassinates those who support U.S. efforts," *The Washington Post*, May 22, 2010, http://www.washingtonpost.com/wp-dyn/content/article/2010/05/21/AR2010052104950.html (accessed 14 October, 2010).
[95] Jeffrey A. Dressler, "Securing Helmand: Understanding and Responding to the Enemy," *Institute for The Study of War,* September 2009, page 4, http://www.understandingwar.org/files/SecuringHelmandPDF.pdf (accessed October 12, 2010).
[96] CJ Radin, "The military strategy in Afghanistan," *The Long War Journal*, February 14, 2010, http://www.longwarjournal.org/archives/2010/02/the_military_strateg.php (accessed 14 October, 2010).

successfully marched into Kandahar, the tribal chiefs loyal to Amir Dost Muhammad fled to the western regions of the country.[97] Similarly, when Dost Muhammad Khan returned to Afghanistan in 1841, he "joined forces with Uzbek Beg of Tashqurghan, Mir Wali."[98]

During Soviet occupation, major uprisings took place in several cities across Afghanistan including Kandahar, Herat, and Jalalabad.[99] While the most prominent anti-Soviet resistance groups operated from Peshawar, several non-Pashtun guerillas fighting from other regions of the country also distinguished themselves in the war. Ahmed Shah Masood, a Tajik, is regarded as "the most effective, and best known, of the *Mujahideen* who fought the Soviet occupation 20 years ago."[100] Ismail Khan, the hero of Herat in western Afghanistan, resisted the Soviets from his city for more than thirteen years until the city became the capital of his mini-kingdom. Abdur Rashid Dostum, a colorful and extremely capable guerilla leader in the anti-Soviet war, made a major contribution as the head of his ethnic Uzbek militia known as Jowjzan.

Summing up, while the treacherous mountains astride Pakistan-Afghanistan border afford important guerilla hideouts, in the end it is the will and the courage of a people that stands between occupation and freedom.

---

[97] William Vogelsang, *The Afghans* (Oxford, UK: Blackwell Publishers Ltd, 2002), 248.
[98] Ibid.
[99] Amstutz, *Afghanistan*, 131.
[100] Jason Burke, "Waiting for a last battle with the Taliban," *The Guardian*, June 27, 1999, http://www.guardian.co.uk/world/1999/jun/27/afghanistan (accessed October 27, 2010).

SECTION-III

Policy Failures

What king, going to encounter another king in war, will not sit down first and take council whether he is able with ten thousand to meet him who comes against him with twenty thousand."[101]

It is difficult to overstate the critical role of policy in leveraging battles and winning wars. While the British excursions in Afghanistan were an outgrowth of an ambitious policy, the failure of policymakers to guide wars to their end is even more pronounced in the so-called Irregular Wars (IW) or Counter-Insurgency (COIN) fights of the Soviet Union and the US-NATO coalition. Ringsmore and Thruelsen believe, "The politically contested and prolonged character of counter-insurgency warfare makes significant demands on the policymakers who are supporting and taking responsibility for the campaign." [102] They further state that this "holds particularly true for democratically elected governments confronted with a war-weary public."[103] This section will explore how myriad failures of policy during the 1st Anglo-Afghan War, the Soviet Invasion, and the US-NATO campaign in that country, ultimately led to the failure of the mission, or a relative lack of success.

A Grand Strategy *sans* Grandeur

Most historians generally agree that the "British concerns over Russia's long-term interests in Afghanistan and points south"[104] became the main cause for 1st Anglo-Afghan War. Any sane British strategy would have therefore sought to enhance British influence in Afghanistan *without* attempting drastic steps that ran the risk of antagonizing public opinion and hurting instead of helping the British interests in this region. Instead of working with and through a perfectly legitimate government in Kabul,

---

[101] Luke, 14.31.

[102] Jens Ringsmose and Peter Dahl Thruelsen, "NATO´s counterinsurgency campaign in Afghanistan: Are classical doctrines suitable for alliances?," *UNISCI Discussion Papers* (January 2010): 61. Available online at http://redalyc.uaemex.mx/pdf/767/76712438005.pdf (accessed October 20, 2010).

[103] Ibid., 62.

[104] Goodson, *Afghanistan's Endless War*, 33.

"the British chose an unusual course" [105] of sweeping aside Amir Dost Muhammad and replacing him with ex-Amir Shah Shuja. This in itself implied commitments beyond initial military victory, and that was something the British neither anticipated nor prepared for.

In the Soviet case, despite the overarching ambition to sustain and perpetuate a satellite state in Afghanistan, the grand strategy hinged on their military strength with a plan to "occupy the main airbases, garrisons, governmental centers and key points, and use aircraft, helicopter-gunships, armored vehicles and artillery, to keep open the roads linking them, assisting the Afghan Army as necessary." [106] Within the span of a single, brutal decade, the Soviets learnt that no amount of military power could keep afloat a strategy devoid of the necessary political compliment. Soviet misadventure in Afghanistan also "reaffirmed the modern proposition that military strength does not necessarily yield political results." [107] The Soviets ended up repeatedly revising their initial goals as military forces struggled to support inexplicably unclear strategies. James Amstutz goes as far as to say that, at least during 1980-84, the Soviets "never developed a successful strategy to pacify the country." [108]

The American mission in Afghanistan started with a simple goal: to dismantle and destroy the al Qaeda network in that country. The relatively small size of the military component of the mission generally conformed to this goal. However, President Bush's curt challenge to the Taliban to hand over the terrorists or share in their fate [109] concealed the grave possibility of a mission creep. The Taliban refused to hand over al Qaeda and ended up becoming America's enemy. A year thereafter, Bush's Secretary of Defense declared "the Taliban are gone….the al Qaeda are gone." [110] As the Bush administration used this false sense of victory to justify treating Afghanistan as "a military and political

---

[105] O'Ballance, *Afghan Wars*, 9.

[106] Ibid., 97.

[107] Tom Rogers, *The Soviet Withdrawal from Afghanistan: Analysis and Chronology* (Westport, Connecticut: Greenwood Press, 1992), 4.

[108] Amstutz, *Afghanistan*, 143.

[109] President George W. Bush, *Address to a Joint Session of Congress and the American People at the United States Capitol Washington, D.C.*, September 20, 2010, http://georgewbush-whitehouse.archives.gov/news/releases/2001/09/20010920-8.html (accessed October 19, 2010)

[110] Seymour M. Hersh, "The Other War: Why Bush's Afghanistan problem won't go away," *The New Yorker*, April 12, 2004, http://www.newyorker.com/archive/2004/04/12/040412fa_fact (accessed October 19, 2010)

backwater—a detour along the road to Iraq,"[111] the strategic error of hyphenating *Pashtun* Taliban with largely Arab al Qaeda came back to haunt the planners of this war.

While the post-Bush political leadership in Washington DC has continued to talk about the "nexus of al Qaeda and the Taliban," [112] they have indeed attempted to come up with what Robert Gates, US Secretary of Defense, has termed as the first real strategy for Afghanistan since the early 1980s.[113] Although the Obama administration has outlined what some call "a more integrated and better resourced political-military approach"[114] in addition to replacing or removing two top Generals in less than two years, the original failure to provide a focused strategic direction to smartly wrap up the work in Afghanistan continues to produce dire ramifications. Despite the fact that this campaign has become the "central part of this administration's foreign policy agenda and, perhaps, its legacy,"[115] the higher direction of war has yet to make its mark.

John Nagl believes that, "the current U.S. campaign is overly ambitious, excessively costly, and doomed to fail."[116] Despite the sacrifices of those fighting on the ground, Nagl goes on to write, "there is decreasing confidence in the body politic that America has a strategy in Afghanistan worthy of the name, that the United States can achieve its goals in Afghanistan at a price in proportion to the expected gain, or that it even knows what it is we are trying to achieve there."[117]

What exactly is wrong with the US-NATO strategy in Afghanistan? While some analysts object to the fundamental assumptions underlying the strategy, for others it is an issue of ditching smart choices and taking up the wrong cause. Simon and Stevenson question whether US strategic interests "actually require the United States to assume the grand and onerous responsibility of rebuilding the Afghan

---

[111] Hersh, "The Other War".

[112] The White House, "Remarks by the President on a New Strategy for Afghanistan and Pakistan," March 27, 2009, available at www.whitehouse.gov/the_press_office/Remarks-by-the-President-on-a-New-Strategy-for-Afghanistan-and-Pakistan/ (accessed October 19, 2010)

[113] Robert Gates, *CNN*, September 27, 2009, http://archives.cnn.com/TRANSCRIPTS/0909/27/sotu.01.html (accessed October 19, 2010)

[114] The White House, "Remarks by the President," March 27, 2009.

[115] John A. Nagl, "A Better War in Afghanistan," *JFQ*, Issue 56 (1st quarter 2010): 32.

[116] Ibid.

[117] Ibid., 33.

state."[118] Retired Colonel Ralph Peters argues America's grand ambition to build an ideal Afghanistan

dilutes its efforts to strike the mortal enemies, mires US forces in a vain mission civilatrice, and leaves

American troops hostage to the whims of venomous regimes.[119] George Friedman thinks what the US is

currently doing, that is protecting the Karzai government and key cities, is "not significantly contributing

to the al Qaeda-suppression strategy."[120]

Under the Obama administration, the focus of attention has shifted to "securing the population

and reducing civilian casualties," [121] just as the soldiers fight an increasingly virulent Taliban insurgency.

The completely avoidable dilemma of treating both Taliban and al Qaeda as a monolithic enemy of the

United States still sits stubbornly at the heart of a US policy divide as "some senior leaders focus on

attacking al Qaeda, while others favor defeating the Taliban as a means of denying al Qaeda its sanctuary

over the long term."[122] A soldier in the wilderness of Helmand can only mourn the dark humor in the

words of US Senator John Kerry during a recent visit to Kabul: "This is the first time we've had a

strategy. People seem to forget that this was only announced last December."[123]

How will history treat this lack of strategic direction in an effort that involves lives of brave

young men and women? While it is not hard to guess the answer, thousands of Americans and Afghans,

richly deserving a joyous life, will have died before a historian honestly writes about how strategists

failed the soldiers.

---

[118] Steven Simon and Jonathan Stevenson, "Afghanistan: How Much is Enough?", Survival, 51: 5 (October-November 2009): 47. Available online at http://pdfserve.informaworld.com/37859_731226487_915362559.pdf (accessed October 19, 2010)

[119] Ralph Peters, "Trapping Ourselves in Afghanistan and Losing Focus on the Essential Mission," *Joint Forces Quarterly* 54 (2009), available online at http://www.army.mil/-news/2009/07/31/25310-trapping-ourselves-in-afghanistan-and-losing-focus-on-the-essential-mission/index.html (accessed September 12, 2010)

[120] George Friedman, "Strategic Divergence: The War Against the Taliban and the War Against Al Qaeda," *Stratfor Global Intelligence*, January 26, 2009,
http://www.stratfor.com/weekly/20090126_strategic_divergence_war_against_taliban_and_war_against_al_qaeda (accessed May 25, 2010)

[121] Christopher J. Lamb and Martin Cinnamond, "Unified Effort: Key to Special Operations and Irregular Warfare in Afghanistan," *Joint Forces Quarterly* 56 (2010): 1. Available online at
http://www.ndu.edu/inss/docUploaded/SF248_Lamb.pdf (accessed October 20, 2010)

[122] Ibid., 2.

[123] Karim Talbi, "US looks to Iraq strategy for Afghanistan," *The China Post*, August 24, 2010,
http://www.chinapost.com.tw/commentary/afp/2010/08/24/269865/US-looks.htm (accessed October 20, 2010)

Of End States and Exit Strategies

The Simla Manifesto of 1838, that pledged a military campaign to dethrone Amir Dost Muhammad and install Shah Shuja, stated that, "the British forces would be withdrawn as soon as this had been accomplished."[124] The fact is that this was indeed accomplished quickly as "the Army of the Indus entered Kabul unopposed on 7 August 1839."[125] The British policy planners lost a valuable opportunity to disengage when, after the fall of Ghazni in July 1839, they rejected Amir Dost Muhammad's emissaries to the British commander suing for peace.[126] However, instead of disengaging quickly and gracefully, the British imperial forces ended up sustaining and defending an incompetent, unpopular, and corrupt regime.

For inexplicable reasons, the British policymakers took up the job of governing an ungovernable country and ended up staying in Kabul as its unannounced viceroys for tens of months after the accomplishment of the initial objectives. With the passage of every month, the resistance picked up its fury and in the end routed the British army as well as their ambition. Due to a lack of policy effort to think right through to the end, "the British suffered major military disasters and when they finally withdrew they left behind them a situation largely indistinguishable from the *status quo ante bellum.*"[127]

The Soviet case was hardly any different. The ambition was to build a progressive, communist satellite state in Afghanistan. Milan Hauner believes, "the immediate political aim of Soviet policy after the invasion was to salvage the Saur Revolution of April 1978 by installing a dependable leadership in Kabul."[128] Moscow's ultimate goal was "to stabilize and Sovietize Afghanistan, so that it would be a

---

[124] O'Ballance, *Afghan Wars,* 10.
[125] Ibid., 13.
[126] O'Ballance, *Afghan Wars,* 13.
[127] Brian Robson, *Crisis on the Frontier: The Third Afghan War and the Campaign in Waziristan 1919-1920* (Staplehurst, Kent: Spellmount Limited, 2004), xi.
[128] Milan Hauner, *The Soviet war in Afghanistan: Patterns of Russian Imperialism* (Lanham, Md: University Press of America, 1991), 114.

stable client state and not a source of threats to the Soviet Union."[129] The initial objectives were achieved quickly as the "Soviet invasion was completely unopposed,"[130] and then they ran out of ideas.

Due to their obsession with military force as the ultimate arbiter of conflicts, no one in Moscow bothered to see in the local rebellions of late 1978 the seeds of a war of national destruction that would change the course of world history.[131] Policy planners seemingly had no time for things like timelines and an exit strategy. As Steve Coll believes, the first real exit strategy from the Soviet war in Afghanistan was evolved by Gorbachev. Coll asserts that, soon after coming to power, Mikhail Gorbachev wanted to pull out of a deteriorating war in Afghanistan but he was "boxed in by hardliners in his Politburo and military."[132] After a decade long directionless effort, "the Soviets began to pull back into Afghanistan's major cities and to "Afghan-ize" their military operations."[133] However, their policy blunders proved too hard to correct by this relatively significant change of course. In the end, Gorbachev felt compelled to let the sacrifices of Soviet military go down the hole. Having run out of any viable options, the Soviets were compelled to just "get out of there."[134]

The United States marched into Afghanistan with a concisely stated but seldom fully understood end state. Also missing was an exit strategy. Ten years into the war, George Friedman believes, "there is (still) no exit strategy."[135] Amidst all the talk of launching a beginning of the end somewhere in the middle of 2011, the situation in Afghanistan has hardly improved from what it was at the start of the campaign. Dan Twining thinks that what Obama administration is calling an exit strategy seems instead to be a political move to buy time and assuage domestic critics while hoping that the success of the mini-

---

[129] Oleg Kulakov, "Lessons learned from the Soviet Intervention in Afghanistan: Implications for Russian Defense Reform," *NATO Defense College, Research Paper No. 26* (March 2006): 2.

[130] O'Ballance, *Afghan Wars,* 91.

[131] Goodson, *Afghanistan's Endless War*, 55.

[132] Steve Coll, "Gorbachev Was Right," *The New Yorker,* September 29, 2009, http://www.newyorker.com/online/blogs/stevecoll/2009/09/gorbachev-was-right.html (accessed October 22, 2010).

[133] Ibid.

[134] Andrew North, "Soviet lessons from Afghanistan," *BBC News*, November 18, 2009, http://news.bbc.co.uk/2/hi/south_asia/8365187.stm (accessed October 22, 2010).

[135] George Friedman, "Now for the Hard Part: From Iraq to Afghanistan," *Stratfor*, July 15, 2008, http://www.stratfor.com/weekly/now_hard_part_iraq_afghanistan (accessed September 20, 2010).

surge will deliver a political and strategic environment conducive to a sustained U.S. military presence beyond 2011.[136]

Ten years after the first bullet of the campaign was fired, Afghanistan is as crippled, factionalized, war-lorded, and violent as it was in the 1980s. Tragically, most of the debate about an exit strategy from Afghanistan focuses on saving the Coalition's face instead of securing the future of Afghanistan. Segbatullah Sanjar, chief policy adviser for Afghan President Hamid Karzai, mourns the failure of policy in leveraging battles towards a stable end: "We couldn't solve the Afghanistan problem in eight years, but now the U.S. wants to solve it in eighteen months? I don't see how it could be done."[137] It is quite clear that policymakers have once again failed to provide a realistic and achievable end-state to the generals.

Resource Crunch: *The Other War* Syndrome

Historical evidence suggests that the British underestimated the challenge and under-resourced the effort during 1st Anglo Afghan War. Alexander Burnes, British envoy to Dost Muhammad's court, thought just "a token escort could ensure the establishment of a client regime."[138] This overdose of confidence reflects the attitude of the British policy planners of the time. Soon after the unopposed conquest of Kabul, "the Army of the Indus was disbanded on 1 January 1840, and only elements remained in Kabul to help Shah Shuja establish himself securely."[139] The deceptive calm caused the British authorities to embark on what some call "a cost cutting exercise."[140] The debilitating exercise

---

[136] Dan Twining, "What is Obama's real 'Exit Strategy' for Afghanistan? And why it matters to India," *Foreign Policy*, December 3, 2009, http://shadow.foreignpolicy.com/posts/2009/12/03/what_is_obamas_real_exit_strategy_for_afghanistan_and_why_it_matters_to_india (accessed October 22, 2010).

[137] Peter Spiegel et al., "Obama Bets Big on Troop Surge," *The Wall Street Journal*, December 2, 2009, http://online.wsj.com/article/SB125967363641871171.html (accessed October 22, 2010).

[138] Jeffery J. Roberts, *The Origins of Conflict in Afghanistan* (Westport, CT: Praeger Publishers, 2003), 5.

[139] O'Ballance, *Afghan Wars,* 13.

[140] Ibid.

included, inter alia, "suspension of subsidies to various Afghan tribes and, more damagingly, inability to relieve the brigade pulled out of Kabul which left behind a seriously depleted garrison."[141]

The Soviet political leadership, their rhetoric notwithstanding, did not accord the requisite focus and resources to the war effort in Afghanistan as "it was felt that the mere presence of Soviet forces would serve to 'sober up' the Mujahideen."[142] While they did not consider Afghanistan a significant military problem, the political effort was never good enough to compliment the work of the military. Because of the prevalent threat perception, a majority of the Soviet military, economic, and political energy went to the European theater and Afghanistan remained on the backburner. According to an official Pentagon estimate of 1989, "the Soviets maintained sixty-eight divisions between their western territories and the NATO frontier" [143] - forces that represented not only the mass of the Soviet Army but its best-trained and best-equipped formations as well.

Economically the Soviet Union was in no position to adequately finance the war effort in Afghanistan. The Soviets suffered from a serious inconsistency between the domestic condition in the Soviet Union and its status as a superpower.[144] Resultantly, "to sustain large forces in Europe, the Kremlin had to abstain from making great commitments elsewhere."[145] Partly in view of Moscow's inability to underwrite the war effort, both the Soviet Chief of General Staff Marshal Ogarkov and his Deputy "voiced strong objections to introducing troops"[146] to the fight in Afghanistan. Having invaded Afghanistan, none of the four General Secretaries of the Central Committee of the Soviet Communist Party who took turns to guide the war effort "could identify a political solution."[147]

---

[141] Ibid., 15.
[142] Grau and Gress, *The Soviet Afghan War*, 72.
[143] Ibid.
[144] Tom Rogers, *The Soviet Withdrawal from Afghanistan: Analysis and Chronology* (Westport, Connecticut: Greenwood Press, 1992), 7.
[145] Rogers, *The Soviet Withdrawal from Afghanistan*, 7.
[146] Savranskaya, "The Soviet Experience in Afghanistan."
[147] Kulakov, "Lessons Learned."

The US-NATO Coalition is no less guilty on account of lack of focus. The US policy in Afghanistan over the past eight years has suffered from what John Nagl calls the most fundamental of all strategic errors: "insufficient resources to accomplish maximalist goals."[148] For a war, which according to estimates of a former top US General in Afghanistan, needed 400,000 troops,[149] the Coalition has been operating mostly with "a woeful lack of manpower and equipment."[150] Quoting senior military and intelligence officials, David Rohde and David Sanger assert, "For the first several years after the collapse of the Taliban regime the Bush Administration ignored Afghanistan almost entirely."[151] Robert Parry mourns the fatal loss of policy focus, "Even as bin Laden and his top lieutenants were cornered in the Afghan mountains at Tora Bora in fall 2001, the attention of Bush and his neocon advisers had already shifted toward Iraq, which the neocons considered a greater threat to Israel's security."[152] The lack of focus afforded the Taliban resistance movement and its allies the much-needed respite to regroup and reorganize.

For a change, President Obama has adopted the Afghanistan effort as "a war of necessity,"[153] contrasting it with "the putative war of choice"[154] in Iraq. However, during the years of neglect, the Taliban and their allies have resurged and, according to a recent report by the Senlis Council, now control vast swathes of unchallenged territory in addition to gaining ever-increasing political legitimacy in the eyes of the Afghan people.[155]

---

[148] Nagl, "A Better War in Afghanistan," 33.

[149] Susanne Koelbl, "The Taliban Kills more Civilians than NATO," *Spiegel International*, September 24, 2007, http://www.spiegel.de/international/world/0,1518,508021,00.html (accessed October 5, 2010)

[150] Ringsmose and Thruelsen, "NATO's counterinsurgency campaign in Afghanistan," 64.

[151] James Dobbins, "Counterinsurgency in Afghanistan - Testimony presented before the House Oversight and Government Reform Committee, Subcommittee on National Security and Foreign Affairs on March 26, 2009," *RAND*, March 23, 2009, http://www.rand.org/pubs/testimonies/CT323/ (accessed October 20, 2010).

[152] Robert Parry, "How Bush Botched the Afghan War," *Baltimore Chronicle and Sentinel*, 27 July 2010, http://baltimorechronicle.com/2010/072710Parry.shtml (accessed October 22, 2010).

[153] Sheryl Gay Stolberg, "Obama Defends Strategy in Afghanistan," *The New York Times*, August 17, 2009, http://www.nytimes.com/2009/08/18/us/politics/18vets.html (accessed October 22, 2010)

[154] Simon and Stevenson, "Afghanistan," 49.

[155] "Taliban control half of Afghanistan, says report," *Telegraph*, UK, November 22, 2007, http://www.telegraph.co.uk/news/worldnews/1570232/Taliban-control-half-of-Afghanistan-says-report.html (accessed October 22, 2010).

In the stories above, who other than the policymakers must carry the blame for messing up a war effort, avoidably prolonging it, and incurring the loss of hundreds of soldiers and tens of thousands of innocent Afghans?

The Annoying Question: Was There a Need to Fight?

As is evident in hindsight, fear instead of a broad-based policy review, was the foundation for the British policy in Afghanistan. In making decisions that involved lives of young men and women and the destiny of a nation, Ellenborough's personal hunches and convictions proved weightier than saner voices of reasons and judgment.[156] In fact, Wellington thought the right thoughts before succumbing to political expediency and approving plans to invade Afghanistan. J.A. Norris records that Wellington believed that while the British in India could easily beat a Russian army of up to 30,000 men moving down from Kabul, "their (British) very presence in Afghanistan would put Britain to enormous military expense."[157] William Vogelsang points out that "both in England and in India, there was strong opposition to the whole affair."[158]

There were others amongst the policymakers who did not even consider it a concern of British foreign policy to see "whether the same objectives could have been obtained with less bloodshed and intrigue."[159] Alexander Burnes, the British envoy to the court of Dost Muhammad Khan reported, "It remains to be considered why we cannot act with Dost Muhammad. He is a man of undoubted ability who has at his heart a high opinion of the British nation."[160] Given the history of successful British intrigue in dethroning several feared rulers in India, it is not far-fetched to believe that the attainment of the British objective - "to depose Amir Dost Muhammad, and to replace him with Shah Shuja"[161] - *was* actually possible without physically invading Afghanistan.

---

[156] Norris, *The First Afghan War*, 27.
[157] Ibid., 30.
[158] William Vogelsang, *The Afghans* (Oxford, UK: Blackwell Publishers Ltd, 2002), 248.
[159] Norris, *The First Afghan War*, xiv.
[160] Jeffery J. Roberts, *The Origins of Conflict in Afghanistan* (Westport, CT: Praeger Publishers, 2003), 4-5.
[161] O'Ballance, *Afghan Wars*, 10.

In the case of the Soviets, introspection over Afghan debacle has taken them years to finally admit, "It never should have been fought."[162] Motivations that inspired Soviet decision to invade Afghanistan had more to do with their paranoia and fears of international isolation than with any real and significant threats emanating from Afghanistan itself. Oleg Kulakov points out that "the decision to send troops to Afghanistan was taken on 12 December 1979, after the Soviet leadership learned about the North Atlantic Council's decision that same day to deploy American medium range missiles in Europe."[163] Quoting Kornienko, Kulakov writes, "There was something emotional in the Soviet decision. It was a way of reacting to the NATO decision."[164]

The war in Afghanistan was yet another evidence of the bankruptcy of Soviet policy and its consequent propensity to repeatedly apply military solutions to essentially political problems. David Isby argues that "the invasion and subsequent involvement has demonstrated that the Soviets can and will use military force to alter political situations on their periphery."[165] Tragically several thousand Soviet soldiers died while "in doubt as to precisely why they were in Afghanistan, having been told they had come to fight the Americans, Chinese or Pakistanis."[166]

While the US motivations for dealing its alleged enemies a blow in Afghanistan may have had more than sufficient emotional and political rationale, the jury is still out on the wisdom of waging a war that would kill thousands of US soldiers and Afghans in pursuit of a few hundred al Qaeda operators. Ralph Peters believes this strategy amounts to "addressing topical symptoms rather than deep causes." [167] The fact that the top US General in Afghanistan, David Petraeus, now backs a reconciliation process[168] between the Karzai regime in Kabul and the Taliban resistance movement, puts a huge question mark on

---

[162] Anthony H. Cordesman and Abraham R. Wagner, *The Lessons of Modern War Vol III: The Afghan and Falklands Conflicts* (London: Mansell Publishing Limited, 1990], 219.
[163] Kulakov, "Lessons Learned."
[164] Kulakov, "Lessons Learned."
[165] Isby, *War in a Distant Country*, 49.
[166] O'Ballance, *Afghan Wars*, 99.
[167] Ralph Peters, "Trapping Ourselves."
[168] "Petraeus backs talks with Taliban," *UPI.com*, September 28, 2010, http://www.upi.com/Top_News/Special/2010/09/28/Petraeus-backs-talks-with-Taliban/UPI-16661285696545/ (accessed October 22, 2010).

the very idea of fighting a full-blown war for so many years. Unfortunately, almost a decade into the war, the policy circles are still divided over whether to continue a counterinsurgency effort against Taliban and al Qaeda, resort to a strategy of more surgical counter-terror strikes, or simply pull out.

The Conflict between Ends and Ways

British policy objectives in Afghanistan of 1830s revolved around "establishing a defensive line well beyond the Indus."[169] This, it was thought for a while, could be achieved by persuading local rulers to accept British advice without direct colonization.[170] Not long thereafter, unfortunately, the policymakers considered the best way to achieve this end was a regime change, that is, to install Shah Shuja in place of Dost Muhammad Khan. This policy over-reach was soon to prove disastrous. The existing Dost Muhammad Khan regime in Kabul was not only competent and legitimate but also willing to extend an olive branch to the British. An astute policy could have worked its way through to the stated 'ends' without any military campaign. Instead, the policymakers adopted a much more costly and long-winded way.

Soviet policy towards Afghanistan drew its inspiration from the so-called Brezhnev Doctrine. One of the tenets of this doctrine gave Soviet Union the self-appropriated right to intervene if any of its client communist regimes was threatened.[171] Afghanistan was, Moscow thought, one ideal place for application of Brezhnev doctrine. However, application was the part that Communists found the hardest of all. Declassified Soviet documents[172] suggest that frequent changes in the mission and mandate baffled the Soviet military. Soon after the troops landed in Kabul, their initial task of protecting the PDPA regime morphed into removing the regime. The military's mandate took yet another turn when the policy planners made the disastrous choice of essentially fighting the Afghan civil war on behalf of their puppets

---

[169] M.J. Gohari, *The Taliban Ascent to Power* (Karachi: Oxford University Press, 2001), 5.
[170] O'Ballance, *Afghan Wars*, 7.
[171] Thomas Taylor Hammond, *Red Flag Over Afghanistan: The Communist Coup, the Soviet Invasion, and the Consequences* (Boulder, Colo: Westview Press, 1984], 132.
[172] Savranskaya, "The Soviet Experience."

in Kabul. These documents also reveal that what started as a surgical military operation soon turned into a bloody counterinsurgency in defense of the Communist ideology.

However, popular support and a complete recasting of Afghan polity were necessary preconditions to achieve the Soviet ideological objectives. Brezhnev thought a regime change or top-down approach would be the right way and therefore he "wanted a friendly, sympathetic Afghan government in Kabul."[173] With hindsight, it is not hard to see that the tyrant's vision was once again wrong and this mistake would cost his empire dearly. Knowing fully that their presence was unwelcome and that the goal of maintaining a client regime in Kabul was untenable, such a government remained the Soviet goal till as late as November 1988.[174] Moscow rulers ignored the conservative and traditionalist nature of Afghan society and, through a coup d'état in April 1978, installed a fledgling communist ruler in place of Mohammad Daoud's nationalist regime.[175] This policy blunder engendered commitments that would keep over a hundred thousand Russian troops mired in a bitter fight against Afghan resistance for over a decade.

In the case of US-NATO, the debate over what should be the realistic objective is still ongoing. Generally, a continuous winding down has been taking place after the initial rhetoric of the Bush years. Here is a sampling of this confusion. Declaring the US objective of preserving Afghanistan's integrity as unrealistic, Simon and Steven believe, the aim should be "merely to ensure that al-Qaeda is denied both Afghanistan and Pakistan as operating bases for transnational attacks on the United States and its allies and partners."[176] While James Dobbins believes the US objectives need to be "more modest,"[177] Jeffrey

---

[173] O'Ballance, *Afghan Wars*, 92.
[174] Isby, *War in a Distant Country*, 49.
[175] Goodson, *Afghanistan's Endless War*, 23.
[176] Simon and Stevenson, "Afghanistan," 50.
[177] Dobbins, "Counterinsurgency in Afghanistan."

Clark takes a clue from Vietnam and concludes that "it was simply beyond the capacity of one power to reform and reshape the society of another."[178]

As the debate over the *right* strategy in Afghanistan rages on, a consensus has been hard to come by. On the one hand are those who believe there are no viable alternatives to a full-bodied counterinsurgency and state-building approach.[179] On the other hand are voices advocating an end state that is "more realistic than a prosperous and modern representative democracy."[180] President Barack Obama, at least for the time being, seems to have leaned towards the counterinsurgency camp. In his speech at West Point in December 2009, he laid out a threefold objective for US-NATO campaign in Afghanistan: "reverse the momentum of the Taliban insurgency, enhance the capacity of the Afghan government and partner with Pakistan."[181]

While all this acrimony over strategy goes on, the situation on the ground has been worsening. The Taliban has not only resurged but Afghanistan itself has lapsed into a largely ungoverned space that produces more than 90 per cent of the world's illicit opium,[182] where former warlords occupy places of prestige and honor,[183] and Taliban are paid off with taxpayers' money.[184] The spontaneous reaction of a photojournalist working in the streets of Afghanistan captures the situation rather starkly: "People always

[178] Jeffrey J. Clark, *Advice & Support: The Final Years 1965-1973* (Washington, DC: U.S. Army Center of Military History, 1988), 521.

[179] Joseph J. Collins, "Afghanistan: The Path to Victory," *JFQ 54* (2009): 58. Available online at http://www.ndu.edu/press/lib/images/jfq-54/16.pdf (accessed October 29, 2010)

[180] Nagl, "A Better War," 34.

[181] William B. Taylor Jr. and J. Alexander Their, "The Road to Successful Transition in Afghanistan: From Here to the December 2010 Review." *United States Institute of Peace*, PeaceBrief No.30, May 12, 2010, http://www.usip.org/node/1726/resources-tools (accessed October 15, 2010).

[182] Mark Dodd , "AFP faces struggles to train Afghans," *The Australian*, October 21, 2010, http://www.theaustralian.com.au/national-affairs/defence/afp-faces-struggles-to-train-afghans/story-e6frg8yo-1225941412641 (accessed October 22, 2010).

[183] "The Other Karzai," *New Zealand Herald*, October 9, 2010, http://www.nzherald.co.nz/world/news/article.cfm?c_id=2&objectid=10679291 (accessed October 22, 2010).

[184] Hamid Shalizi, "Afghans pay off Taliban with 'American money," *Reuters*, October 13, 2010, http://www.msnbc.msn.com/id/39646568/ns/world_news-south_and_central_asia/ (accessed October 22, 2010).

ask me broad policy questions—most of all, how the US can win in Afghanistan. After four years there, I'm forced to ask: *what is there to win?*"[185]

What Kind of War Is It?

The British imperial forces were clearly not prepared for what was coming. Initially out to wage a campaign of violence to defeat an existing regime, the decision makers ended up establishing garrisons, brought up their families and sought to lead a life of comfort in a land they had just trampled under their feet. The historical evidence suggests that British garrisons in Kabul and Jalalabad were completely unprepared for the fierce hordes of Afghan resistance that descended on them. After months of debilitating defensive maneuvers, the feared British imperial forces that shook the spine of Afghan resistance just a few years prior, retreated from Afghanistan like a convoy of trekkers and picnickers in which children and women outnumbered the fighting men. Their example was a classic case of poor policy incapacitating the fighting spirit of soldiers.

Going by their preparations and wherewithal, the Soviet military forces invading Afghanistan expected to fight pitched battles against a large conventional force. Organized and indoctrinated to fight conventional wars against sophisticated enemies on a European battlefield, the Soviet policymakers failed to work with their senior military leaders to prepare their men for the nature of war in Afghanistan. Resultantly, the Soviet military "arrived with their full complement of tanks, arms, and equipment for such a (conventional, sophisticated) conflict, and were at once out of their elements in the mountainous, largely barren Afghanistan."[186] Russian soldiers "knew remarkably little about the enemy, meaning the 'rebels'."[187] As they encountered the "ominous glares that had once greeted the Grand Army of the Indus,"[188] the Soviets discovered that Kabul was a place different from Budapest or Prague.

---

[185]Louie Palu, *Total War,* VQR, Spring 2010, http://www.vqronline.org/articles/2010/spring/palu-total-war/ (accessed October 2, 2010).

[186] O'Ballance, *Afghan Wars,* 97.

[187] Ibid., 100.

[188] Stephen Tanner, *Afghanistan: A Military History from Alexander the Great to the War Against the Taliban* (Da Capo Press, 2002), 241.

After their disastrous Spring Offensive in 1980, the Soviet military did try a course correction and consulted their allies in Vietnam on successful ways to counter resistance tactics. However, the senior Soviet leadership, especially Marshall Sokolov, had other thoughts and rejected out of hand the Vietnamese recommendations to "use small sub-units of Special Forces, supported and supplied by helicopters."[189] Most of the senior Soviet leadership "had an inherent dislike of guerilla warfare"[190] and it cost their men dearly. However, after a spate of embarrassing losses, by late 1983, Soviets lost faith in conventional tactics. Thereafter, they mostly resorted to punitive operations and no longer sought to seize and hold territory.[191] The possibility of a negotiated peace or a political solution faded with increase in military brutalities. Due to the abject failure of policy to guide and regulate military effort towards a political end, the reverse trends took hold of the situation with every passing year.

In the US, policy circles are still divided over what kind of war to fight in Afghanistan. The discord between those who advocate a full-blown Counterinsurgency effort and the proponents of a more neat, more precise and manpower-effective Counter-terrorism (CT) strategy is hitherto unresolved. The champions of CT strategy believe there is no "insurgency in Afghanistan; rather, it is a civil war."[192] Counter-terror pundits also believe that "a deeply committed counterinsurgency campaign in Afghanistan is potentially counterproductive, probably unwinnable, and in any event unnecessary."[193] George Friedman is one such pundit who thinks that the search for al Qaeda and other Islamist groups is "an intelligence matter best left to the covert capabilities of U.S. intelligence and Special Operations Command."[194]

---

[189] O'Ballance, *Afghan Wars*, 101.
[190] Ibid.
[191] Ibid., 119.
[192] Warner, "Context and What's Next," 19.
[193] Simon and Stevenson, "Afghanistan," 65.
[194] George Friedman, "Strategic Divergence: The War Against the Taliban and the War Against Al Qaeda," *Stratfor*, January 26, 2009, http://www.stratfor.com/weekly/20090126_strategic_divergence_war_against_taliban_and_war_against_al_qaeda (accessed October 20, 2010)

Those supporting an extended COIN campaign, on the other hand, note that "the Taliban is not a unified or monolithic movement, that many Taliban militants fight for reasons having nothing to do with Islamic zealotry, and that each Taliban grouping has specific needs and particular characteristics."[195] The *COINdinistas,*[196] a term used for the brains that have made counterinsurgency the centerpiece of the world's most powerful military, believe, "The theory of victory lies in a competition for effective rule and legitimacy -- local political outcomes that are enabled by, yet distressingly independent of, military success."[197]

While a debate like this is a sign of healthy learning environment within an organization, the fact that it has gone on inconclusively for over a decade now, has not added any clarity to situation on the ground. A Washington Post editorial, quoting Bob Woodward, points out, "Many of the president's senior White House advisers believe that the modified counterinsurgency strategy he adopted last year is doomed to fail -- and some suspect the president shares their views."[198] However impressive may be the range of euphemisms used to describe this divide, the fact remains that it represents policy's signal failure to bring the much-needed clarity to the campaign.

The Credibility Gap: *Betting on the Wrong Horses*

Succeeding foreign missions in Afghanistan have preferred to operate through what Barnett Rubin calls "a westernized patrimonial patronage network in Kabul,"[199] who sustain their ties with the Afghan society by distributing the largesse coming from their foreign patrons. Historically the *Qalang* elite in Kabul have been overly willing to serve foreign masters. Their services have however seldom

---

[195] Fotini Christia and Michael Semple, 'Flipping the Taliban', *Foreign Affairs*, 88-4, (July–August 2009): 40-41. Available online at http://www.foreignaffairs.com/articles/65151/fotini-christia-and-michael-semple/flipping-the-taliban (accessed October 4, 2010).

[196] Thomas E. Ricks, "The COINdinistas," *Foreign Policy*, December 1, 2009, http://www.foreignpolicy.com/articles/2009/11/30/the_coindinistas (accessed October 22, 2010).

[197] Eliot A. Cohen, "Obama's COIN toss," *The Washington Post*, December 6, 2009, http://www.washingtonpost.com/wp-dyn/content/article/2009/12/04/AR2009120402602.html (accessed October 22, 2010).

[198] "Bob Woodward's book portrays a great divide over Afghanistan," *The Washington Post*, September 29, 2010, http://www.washingtonpost.com/wp-dyn/content/article/2010/09/28/AR2010092805200.html (accessed October 22, 2010).

[199] Rubin, *The Fragmentation of Afghanistan*, 21.

delivered any good either to their masters or to the Afghan nation. Barnett Rubin further writes that instead of working to incorporate the population into a common national political system, "the political elite (has invariably) acted as an ethnically stratified hierarchy of intermediaries between the foreign powers providing the resources and the groups receiving the largesse of patronage."[200]

In the case of the British, installing the unpopular Shah Shuja was easily one of the worst decisions around that period.[201] Although the British puppet Shah Shuja was a Sadozai *Pashtun*,[202] foreign support destroyed his credibility in the eyes of his fellow tribesmen. Larry Goodson supports this: "Being placed as a pro-British puppet on the throne in Kabul by force of arms automatically discredited him, whatever his previous position or current standing in *Pashtun* tribal politics might have been."[203]

The Soviets did not heed the lesson British learnt from installing their puppet.[204] Historical evidence suggests that the Afghan struggle in the 1980s was as much against Soviet presence as against the unpopular puppets installed in Kabul. As early as in 1978, "the vast majority of Afghans saw the *Khalq* program as anti-Islamic actions by a regime that now also appeared to be a tool of foreign 'infidels'."[205] Even the Afghan armed forces were discredited by the fact that they were trained by the Soviets.[206] As the new government brought to Afghanistan from the Soviet Union,[207] started consolidating its power with the help of its puppeteers in Moscow, the Afghan street sentiment against it kept rising. As quickly as in early 1979, "most of Afghanistan was in open revolt against the Khalq (communist) government."[208] The nationwide sentiment against foreign presence and control of Afghan

---

[200] Rubin, *The Fragmentation of Afghanistan*, 20.
[201] O'Ballance, *Afghan Wars*, 9.
[202] Ibid., 8.
[203] Goodson, *Afghanistan's Endless War*, 33.
[204] Ibid.
[205] Isby, *War in a Distant Country*, 19.
[206] O'Ballance, *Afghan Wars*, 97.
[207] Kulakov, "Lessons learned."
[208] Goodson, *Afghanistan's Endless War*, 57.

affairs turned into a national revolution against the Parchami puppet government and its Soviet supporters.[209]

The fate of the last Soviet puppet in Afghanistan, Dr Najibullah – a Pashtun from a respected clan - is also a poignant reminder of Afghan hostility towards regimes acting on behalf and at the behest of foreigners. As soon as the Soviets left Afghanistan, Najib was reduced to, in the words of a former anti-Soviet guerilla, "a suspended tear drop, about to fall."[210] It was not long before the world saw the rather sad sight of the bodies of Najib and his brother, strung up by their necks from an elevated traffic island just outside the imposing building of their Presidential Palace. [211]

Presumably, with little time to take note of the lessons of history, the US-NATO coalition marched headlong into the first part of an oft-repeated and disastrous plan: installing a puppet in Kabul. Soon after the ouster of Taliban from Kabul, the US sought to limit its own involvement by working with and through militia or tribal commanders to provide security and mop up the remaining al Qaeda presence.[212] This approach "empowered these commanders to act abusively and unaccountably.... and thereby facilitated the Taliban's reemergence as an insurgency against the new government and international presence."[213] Thereon, the US and its Kabul puppets have mutually reinforced each other's lack of credibility in the eyes of the Afghans. Volney Warner recounts that most of the Afghans he spoke with barely acknowledged, if at all, President [Hamid] Karzai as other than a Western puppet and that whatever he embraced, the people would not.[214]

Much like the British and the Soviet stooges, the US puppet in Kabul has been little short of a disaster for US credibility and legitimacy. Johnson and Mason believe that the massive rigging of elections in August 2009 has "merely shifted Afghan public perception of Karzai from contempt to

---

[209] Goodson, *Afghanistan's Endless War*, 59.
[210] Michael Griffin, *Reaping the Whirlwind: The Taliban Movement in Afghanistan* (London: Pluto Press, 2001), 1.
[211] Ibid.
[212] Nagl, "A Better War," 34.
[213] Antonio Giustozzi, *Koran, Kalashnikov,and Laptop: The Neo-Taliban Insurgency in Afghanistan* (New York: Columbia University Press, 2008), 15–21.
[214] Warner, "Context and What's Next," 22.

scorn."[215] Much like other puppets in the past, the US choice has increasingly become a problem,[216] and western allies increasingly feel they are "stuck with him."[217]

Nikolas Gvosdev believes it is time to raise the following question, "Is Afghan President Hamid Karzai another Babrak Karmal, who was the Soviet Union's initial preference as Afghanistan's leader but who was unable to build a self-supporting regime that permitted his foreign benefactors to go home?"[218] As frustration with Kazai regime's incompetence and corruption grows, the resistance to US presence will only intensify pushing an honorable exit from Afghanistan even further away.

Strategic Drift to Mission Creep

The fact that the British Army of Indus included some 20,000 troops and more than 40,000 camp followers reflected the mindset of those who planned this invasion. Much like the British ambition to install a pliable puppet in Kabul, the Soviets under Brezhnev "just wanted a friendly, sympathetic Afghan government on (Soviet Union's) southern border."[219] This simple Russian mission was to soon morph into a plan for complete transformation of Afghan state and society; an objective involving a long-term commitment with little assurance of success. Militarily, the Soviets "did not expect to fight but just to provide firepower back-up for the Afghan Army, which would combat rebels on the ground."[220] This lack of clarity in policy objectives ended up embroiling the Soviet military in a painfully long and, in the end, fruitless effort.

---

[215] Thomas H. Johnson and M. Chris Mason, "Refighting the Last War: Afghanistan and the Vietnam Template," *Military Review*, (November-December 2009): 4. Available online at http://usacac.army.mil/cac2/militaryreview/archives/english/militaryreview_20091231_art004.pdf (accessed September 15, 2010).

[216] Jackson Diehl, "Obama's Karzai problem," *The Washington Post*, February 24, 2010, http://voices.washingtonpost.com/postpartisan/2010/02/karzai.html (accessed October 22, 2010).

[217] Alissa J. Rubin, "Karzai's Words Leave Few Choices for the West," *The New York Times*, April 4, 2010, http://www.nytimes.com/2010/04/05/world/asia/05karzai.html (accessed October 22, 2010).

[218] Nikolas K. Gvosdev, The Soviet Victory that Never Was, *Foreign Affairs*, December 10, 2010, http://www.foreignaffairs.com/articles/65713/nikolas-k-gvosdev/the-soviet-victory-that-never-was?page=2 (accessed October 22, 2010).

[219] O'Ballance, *Afghan Wars*, 92.

[220] Ibid., 97.

The US-NATO mission is no different in this regard. Ann Tyson, in a scathing criticism of the conduct of war in Afghanistan, [221] argues that Bonn Agreement and subsequent accords have expanded Afghan and coalition aims far beyond the original objective of toppling the Taliban government and defeating al Qaeda. After 8 years of what Ms Tyson calls a "strategic drift," [222] coalition efforts have failed to persuade many Afghans that it is safe to defy the Taliban and commit themselves to the Coalition and Kabul regime. Volney Warner goes so far as to suggest that policy planners have tended to "fan the flames of continued involvement, not for reason of national objectives but to perpetuate their COIN cause." [223]

Right from its conception stages, the war in Afghanistan has been deeply political. Based on the events and rhetoric of the initial few months, it seems the political leadership of the time wanted to use this spectacular show of force as a means to look strong and determined. That it ended up mired in a crisis that refuses to end is another part of the story. Soon after the initial successes, preservation of pride became a foundation of policy. As Secretary of Defense Robert Gates reminded us, "To fail - or to be seen to fail - in either Iraq or Afghanistan would be a disastrous blow to U.S. credibility, both among friends and allies, and among potential adversaries." [224] He had, sadly enough, very few ideas on how to succeed. Volney Warner believes that the administration actually detoured from the original objective and "exploited the public's 9/11 outrage and fears to pursue other political agendas....under the rubric of a war on terror." [225] Tragically, even if there is a rush of humility after years of a blinding hubris, a winding back to the original mission of this war sounds like a defeat.

---

[221] Ann Scott Tyson, "In Helmand, Caught between U.S., Taliban; 'Skittish' Afghans Wary of Both Sides," *The Washington Post*, August 15, 2009, http://www.washingtonpost.com/wp-dyn/content/article/2009/08/14/AR2009081403568.html (accessed October 20, 2010).
[222] Ibid.
[223] Warner, "Context and What's Next," 19.
[224] Robert M. Gates, "A Balanced Strategy: Reprogramming the Pentagon for a New Age," *Foreign Affairs* 88, Number 1 (January-February 2009). Available online at http://web.ebscohost.com/ehost/detail?vid=7&hid=106&sid=028e9f71-84b8-4e24-971d-c4191b964831%40sessionmgr104&bdata=JnNpdGU9ZWhvc3QtbGl2ZQ%3d%3d#db=aph&AN=35634218.
[225] Warner, "Context and What's Next," 20.

Governance: The Achilles Heel

In classical counterinsurgency, it is now a truism that "a government that is losing to an insurgency is not being outfought, it is being outgoverned."[226] The only evidence that suggests the British gave some thought to the post-war work comes from the fact that William McNaughton accompanied the Army of Indus as Envoy and Minister on the part of the Government of India at the Court of Shah Shuja.[227] The British also built a cantonment in Kabul and entrenched themselves at various other places in Afghanistan including Bamiyan, Charikar, Qalat-e-Ghilzay, Qandahar, and Jalalabad.[228] However, the British administrative apparatus proved woefully inadequate and, resultantly, most of the affairs of the state and governance were left to the soldiers of the queen. Right from the beginning "the political authorities were overconfident and neglected warnings"[229] of simmering discontent and revolt. The result was utter chaos.

Initially aiming only to support a pliant regime, the Soviets increasingly had to run the day to day affairs of the state of Afghanistan.[230] However, due to lack of requisite capacity and legitimacy, most of rural Afghanistan - more than 75 percent of the country – stayed mostly under the control of the resistance movement.[231] In the end, direct Soviet involvement in law enforcement and governance hurt more than it helped Kabul as it "simply increased the existing hostility of the majority against the PDPA regime and its collaborator."[232] Admitting their failure at governance, Marshal Akhromeyev remarked in 1986, "We

---

[226] David Kilcullen, *The Accidental Guerrilla: Fighting a Small War in the Midst of a Big One* (London: Hurst & Company), 60.
[227] William Vogelsang, *The Afghans* (Oxford, UK: Blackwell Publishers Ltd, 2002), 248.
[228] Ibid.
[229] Hugh Chisholm, *Encyclopedia Britannica* (Eleventh Edition, Published 1910-11), Library of Fogg Museum of Art, Harvard University, accessed scanned version online at http://books.google.com/books on October 22, 2010.
[230] Goodson, *Afghanistan's Endless War*, 63.
[231] Ibid., 60.
[232] O'Ballance, *Afghan Wars*, 97.

control Kabul and the provincial centers, but…we have lost the battle for the Afghan people."[233] He also

believed that the main problem was a lack of political follow-up to military actions.[234]

The US-NATO coalition has not fared any better than the Soviets. Writing in Joint Forces

Quarterly, Joseph Collins notes that "the major mistake made by the coalition has been the failure to build

Afghan capacity for governance, rule of law, and security."[235] The community leaders warned President

Hamid Karzai during a visit to Marjah, a Taliban controlled town in Helmand province, that the Taliban

were popular there precisely because his *government* was so unpopular.[236] General David Petraeus, the

top US General in Afghanistan, has warned that the Taliban were not the only enemy of the people and

that the people were also "threatened by inadequate governance, corruption, and abuse of power."[237] As

soldiers fight the ever so fervent *Pashtun* insurgency, corruption and incompetence of those running the

state from Kabul, both Afghans as well as foreign political managers, continue to undercut the chances of

the ultimate success.

As the Coalition plans to transition administrative responsibilities to the regime in Kabul,

observers warn of the "rising perceptions of Hamid Karzai's government as ineffectual and corrupt." [238]

After almost a decade of the Coalition presence, notes a renowned photojournalist, "Kabul is a chaotic

city of three million mostly impoverished people….(and) a tottering government that can no longer

---

[233] Michael Dobbs, "The Afghan Archive: Secret Memos Trace Kremlin's March to War," *The Washington Post*, 15 November 1992, http://www.encyclopedia.com/The+Washington+Post/publications.aspx?date=19921115&pageNumber=1 (accessed on October 21, 2010 at)

[234] Andrew North, "Soviet lessons from Afghanistan," *BBC News*, November 18, 2009, http://news.bbc.co.uk/2/hi/south_asia/8365187.stm (accessed October 22, 2010)

[235] Collins, "Afghanistan."

[236] Taylor and Their, "The Road to Successful Transition."

[237] General David H. Petraeus, Commander International Security Assistance Force/ United States Forces-Afghanistan COMISAF's Counterinsurgency Guidance, 1 August 2010, issued by HQ ISAF/US Forces-Afghanistan, Kabul, Afghanistan COMISAF/CDR USFOR-A. Available online at http://www.isaf.nato.int/from-the-commander/from-the-commander/comisaf-s-counterinsurgency-guidance.html

[238] Simon and Stevenson "Afghanistan," 51.

provide security."[239] Towards the end of the US-NATO Mission in Afghanistan, good governance still seems to be far off on the horizon.

The Pakistan "Problem"

Interestingly, all three cases under review in this paper also share this problem: the issue of dealing with the *Pashtun* tribesmen in what is now the Federally Administered Tribal Area of Pakistan. Although not directly involved in the resistance against Shah Shuja or the British Army of the Indus, the tribesmen of this area posed considerable problems to the British during their rule in the Indian sub-continent. During the British wars in Afghanistan and tribal area campaigns of 1919-20, tribesmen east of what is now the border between Afghanistan and Pakistan gained a reputation as "probably the most formidable fighting men on the Frontier…fiercely independent, their fighting skills honed by centuries of raiding."[240]

Like their predecessors in Afghanistan's troubled history, the Soviet invaders "found the eastern mountains the hornet's nest of enemy resistance."[241] Since these mountains and their dwellers shared the lands and traditions across areas that are part of Pakistan, the latter inevitably became a stakeholder in the conflict. As Tom Rogers put it, "With millions of Afghan refugees camped inside Pakistan for decades now and with close tribal affinities that straddle the Durand Line, Pakistan was forced to play the role of a direct party during Afghan resistance against Soviets."[242] The United States' role in supporting Afghan freedom struggle from bases inside Pakistan is clear beyond any want of evidence. The Soviets and their successors in Moscow have seldom taken kindly to that role and have since carried a grudge against Pakistan.

---

[239] J. Malcolm Garcia, *"Most Dangerous, Most Unmerciful," VQR* (Spring 2010), http://www.vqronline.org/articles/2010/spring/garcia-most-dangerous/ (accessed October 1, 2010).
[240] Brian Robson, *Crisis on the Frontier: The Third Afghan War and the Campaign in Waziristan 1919-20* (Gloucestershire: Spellmount, 07), 149.
[241] Stephen Tanner, *Afghanistan*, 246.
[242] Tom Rogers, *The Soviet Withdrawal from Afghanistan: Analysis and Chronology* (Westport, Connecticut: Greenwood Press, 1992), 19-22.

However, after the Soviet retreat, the United States' precipitous departure and acrimonious disengagement from the region dealt a massive blow to stability in the area. Soon after the Soviet withdrawal, "the United States curtailed virtually all of its assistance to Pakistan and was perceived by a generation of Pakistani leaders as having abandoned the region." [243] Not long after the end of the Soviet operations in Afghanistan, the US decided to "impose sanctions and ban military-to-military exchanges with Pakistan over its nuclear weapons programs and tests"[244] – activities that the US had conveniently ignored throughout much of the 1980s. While Pakistan's military and political elite mourned it with some bitterness, the US policymakers thus lost their "most significant sources of understanding and levers of influence over events in the region for a generation."[245]

Throughout the ongoing war in Afghanistan, the US has criticized Pakistan for not doing enough to support the war effort in Afghanistan. Pakistan, for its part, believes it has sacrificed more men and achieved more real and solid victories than the US-led coalition operating inside Afghanistan. Regardless of the bickering, it is clear that, of all the neighbors of Afghanistan, Pakistan has been 'condemned' to a position of 'damned if you do and damned if you don't.'

While generally the debate about cross-border violence revolves around how tribes and territories inside Pakistan affect the situation in Afghanistan, Pakistanis complain that few pay heed to how Afghanistan has become a festering sore for the neighborhood, including Pakistan, and how mayhem inside Afghanistan casts its shadows across the wider region. Take for example the phenomenon of *Talibanization*. Opining on Afghanistan's insalubrious effects on the its neighborhood, Larry Goodson writes, "The growing *Talibanization* of Pakistan (that is the application of Taliban social policies and interpretations of Islamic laws in the narrow tribal belt of north western Pakistan) and the increasing

---

[243] Nagl, "A Better War in Afghanistan."
[244] Ibid.
[245] Hussain Haqqani, *Pakistan: Between Mosque and Military* (Washington, DC: Carnegie Endowment for International Peace, 2005), 288.

Islamization of Central Asia highlight the way in which state failure in one country can infect its neighbors."[246]

John Nagl believes that the "problem (of Taliban violence) runs both ways: a failed Afghanistan would become a base from which Taliban and al Qaeda militants could work to further destabilize the surrounding region."[247] Much like the Soviets, the US-led Coalition has apparently been unable, or unwilling, to understand that the situation in Pakistan's tribal belt is an effect, not a cause, of the situation in Afghanistan. Much like the Soviets, the US-led coalition will have to realize, sooner rather than later, that the road between Kabul and Peshawar is a thoroughfare and that all that comes east on this road must one-day return to Kabul.

The Lost Battles of Hearts and Minds

Despite all the pretenses of benevolence, those who organized the British Army of the Indus for invasion of Afghanistan knew that the Empire was about to wage "a war of robbery…a new crime in the annals of nations."[248] In a fascinating chronicle of this war, Jeffrey Robert identifies the root cause of the British unpopularity with the Afghans: "From the beginning of the occupation, the Kabulis regarded the occupying forces with undisguised contempt. Shuja, viewed as a *watan ferosh* (literally "country seller" or traitor), from his arrival, attracted little support."[249] The British thus lost the battle for Afghan hearts before they even began.

The Soviets packaged their public relations pills in both Rubles as well as rubble. As for the Rubles part, by 1978, the Soviets had completed seventy-one separate projects, of which fifty-two were still being operated by Soviet technicians. [250] They had agreed to undertake another sixty projects involving an investment of more than 3 billion dollars. Long before they ever sent a soldier over the

---

[246] Goodson, *Afghanistan's Endless War*, 22.
[247] Nagl, "A Better War in Afghanistan," 33.
[248] David Loyn, *In Afghanistan: Two Hundred Years of British, Russian and American Occupation* (New York: Pelgrave MacMillan, 2009), 27.
[249] Roberts, *"The Origins of Conflict in Afghanistan,"* 6.
[250] Goodson, *Afghanistan's Endless War*, 49-50.

border, the Soviet presence in Afghanistan was already overpowering.[251] However, with the invasion

begun the hard work of convincing Afghans to abandon their freedom in exchange for all the money

Soviets were willing to spend in their country. Billions of dollars in developmental aid, massive people to

people contacts and radio programs to explain the 'noble' intent of the Soviet mission were all washed

away in the end by "brutal military actions like 'rubbleization', 'blanket bombing' and 'starvation

policy'."[252]

Beyond the rhetoric of partnership with the Afghans, the US-led coalition has been losing Afghan

hearts, and fast. As Johnson and Mason put it,"The United States is losing the war in Afghanistan one

Pashtun village at a time, bursting into schoolyards filled with children with guns bristling, kicking in

village doors, searching women, speeding down city streets, and putting out cross-cultural gibberish in

totally ineffectual information operations and psychological operations campaigns - all of which are

anathema to the Afghans."[253] Although US General Stanley Mc Chrystal ostensibly tried hard to stem the

trend, U.S. forces have attracted substantial criticism for "excessive and insufficiently discriminating use

of airstrikes, which have caused significant loss of civilian life."[254] After years of hard work and even

harder fighting, here is what a knowledgeable American wrote in the Joint Forces Quarterly, "Do not

make our Western sense of justice or government a precondition; virtually all Afghans I have spoken with

want us out and that means Western influence, not just troops."[255]

On the positive side, the last two top US Generals have sent out the right messages. General

McChrystal defended his policy of imposing stricter restraint standards in following words, "Winning

hearts and minds in COIN is a coldblooded thing." [256] He based his calculation on the fact that "the

---

[251] Ibid.
[252] O'Ballance, *Afghan Wars*, 99-107.
[253] Thomas H. Johnson and M. Chris Mason, "Understanding the Taliban and Insurgency in Afghanistan," *Orbis* 51 (Winter 2007): 88. Accessed online on September 23, 2010 at http://www.fpri.org/orbis/5101/
[254] Nagle, "A Better War in Afghanistan," 36.
[255] Warner, "Context and What's Next," 23.
[256] C. J. Chivers, "General Faces Unease Among His Own Troops, Too," *The New York Times*, June 22, 2010, http://www.nytimes.com/2010/06/23/world/asia/23troops.html (accessed August 31, 2010).

Russians killed one million Afghans, and that didn't work."[257] His successor General David H. Petraeus reinforced this theme by declaring human terrain as decisive.[258] Through his latest directive, Petraeus has emphasized that "only by providing (to the people) security and earning their trust and confidence can the Afghan government and ISAF prevail."[259] The problem is that, historically, an *occupation* force cannot win Afghan hearts just by holding fire.

Buying Peace: The Hard Work of Reconciliation

One of the most prominent trends in Afghan tribal history has been one of short-term alliances between traditional enemies in the face of a common external threat.[260] Afghans have repeatedly shown a rare ability to fight simultaneous fights: several small tribal fights among themselves and the other big national fight together against the foreigners. This explains why the British failed to buy them into subservience. Historical evidence suggests that the British did actually make payments to certain tribes in return for maintaining peaceful behavior and allow safe passage to British traffic through their areas.[261] However, the unrestrained bloodletting during the dying moments of the British presence in Afghanistan amply proves that this idea failed miserably.

The Soviets also tried to co-opt *Mujahideen* into the Najib government but the guerillas refused to share room with the people they considered as traitors. Several Soviet overtures failed to entice resistance fighters away from their agenda. Najibullah's futile attempt in May 1987 to form a "national reconciliation" government followed a meaningless declaration of a unilateral ceasefire in January 1987.[262] These moves were in addition to massive efforts the Soviets made to buy or bully opponents into some kind of accommodation. Underlying the failure of all these efforts was the sense of shame that most Afghans felt in dealing with the occupiers.

---

[257] Ibid.
[258] General Petraeus, "COMISAF's Counterinsurgency Guidance."
[259] Ibid.
[260] Goodson, *Afghanistan's Endless War*, 26.
[261] Ibid., 38.
[262] Ibid., 69.

After maintaining a stern opposition to any deals with the Taliban and even criticizing neighboring Pakistan for talking several militants into peace, the US-led coalition now seems willing to reconcile with the militants. Here is how a Time Magazine correspondent put this change of heart: "What was once anathema — talking to an enemy that was overthrown by U.S. forces in 2001 in retaliation for sheltering Osama bin Laden's al-Qaeda network — is now gaining acceptance, as the generals realize that military tactics alone will not win this war."[263] However, without achieving genuine socio-economic breakthroughs or breaking the backbone of the resistance – two possibilities that seem equally distant – these overtures are not likely to be any better than their Soviet equivalents. John Nagl believes that flipping less committed insurgents was not likely to help the US achieve a modicum of security on the cheap.[264]

Any disingenuous attempts to divide the resistance will only vitiate trust and hurt whatever chances there are of peace in the near future. An insincere gesture will only damage the Coalition's credibility. It is also a fact that Taliban have come to increasingly represent the wider, almost countrywide anti-occupation sentiment and, so far, "no visible daylight has emerged between the 'good' Taliban and 'bad' militants."[265] An attempt to create imaginary divisions will only vitiate the environment further.

Michael O'Hanlon emphasizes that a reconciliation process must be comprehensive because, in the past, "insufficient political reconciliation process that fails to include various elements of the insurgency has only fueled instability in the country."[266] A sincere reconciliation will have to be wide-ranging and will inevitably involve rolling back all the hate mongering, the demonization, the concoctions, the lies, and the misrepresentations of 'the enemy.' Unfortunately, this is something that

---

[263] Aryn Baker, "Talking with the Taliban: Easier Said Than Done," *Time Magazine*, November 30, 2009, http://www.time.com/time/magazine/article/0,9171,1940679,00.html (accessed October 25, 2010).
[264] Nagle, "A Better War in Afghanistan," 37.
[265] Steven and Stevenson, "Afghanistan," 52.
[266] Michael O'Hanlon, "Toward Reconciliation in Afghanistan," *The Washington Quarterly 32:2* (April 2009): 143. Available online at http://www.twq.com/09april/docs/09apr_OHanlon.pdf (accessed October 15, 2010).

cannot happen without unraveling and exposing the entire narrative built around the so-called global war on terror.

Choosing the Wrong Enemy?

It should now be amply clear to the reader that the British could have achieved their strategic objectives without necessarily contracting the animosity of the Afghans and their revered leader Dost Muhammad Khan. In the Soviet case, troops seldom had a clear idea of who their enemy was going to be. Their leaders had indicated nations as disparate as Chinese, Americans, and Pakistanis as the enemy. Despite all their efforts, the Soviets, according to Lester Grau, "did not understand who they were fighting."[267]

The US-NATO case is scarcely different. Many leading US analysts have alluded to a seemingly mistaken view of the enemy in Afghanistan. Volney Warner believes the "politicians morphed the pursuit of Osama bin Laden into this war, and we included the Taliban in our definition of enemies."[268] While pointing out that none of the 9/11 terrorists was an Afghan, Ralph Peters believes that "even a return to power of the Taliban - certainly undesirable in human-rights terms - does not mean that September 11, Part Two, then becomes inevitable." [269]

Alienation of most of the *Pashtuns*, especially the warlike *Qalang* tribes of the east and south, has been perhaps the most dangerous consequence of contracting Taliban as an enemy. Of all the ethnic groups in Afghanistan, *Pashtuns* are the worst enemy to have. The British Army of the Indus during first Anglo-Afghan War was hit the hardest by, primarily, Ghilzai Pashtuns of the east and southeast.[270] The main resistance front against the Soviets, called "The Peshawar Seven,"[271] recruited predominantly from ethnic *Pashtuns*. It is hard to mistake "the shared *Pashtun* ethnicity of the Taliban and the majority of the

---

[267] Grau and Gress, *"The Soviet Afghan War"*, 72.
[268] Warner, "Context and What's Next," 20.
[269] Ralph Peters, "Trapping Ourselves"
[270] Goodson, *Afghanistan's Endless War*, 33.
[271] O'Ballance, *Afghan Wars*, 115.

non-combatant population in most of the areas they have come to control."[272] Like it or not, Taliban do represent at least the aspiration, if not the socio-religious outlook, of most of the *Pashtuns*. That unfortunately also means majority of the hearts and minds coalition is trying to win.

Even if the main reason for attacking Taliban was to punish them for hosting al Qaeda, George Freedman believes, "that reason might be moot now as al Qaeda appears to be wrecked."[273] A recent statement of CIA Director Leon Panetta claiming the remaining al Qaeda members in Afghanistan may be around "50 to 100, maybe less,"[274] proves that the decade long campaign has managed to considerably degrade the Taliban's 'guests'. In the light of this, George Friedman advocates a rethink on *maintaining* Taliban as an enemy.[275] A recent Stratfor report also asserts al Qaeda has been damaged beyond immediate repair and that it is now in no position to replicate the sort of strategic challenge it did with the 9/11 attacks.[276]

It is amply clear that, unlike al Qaeda, the Taliban do not have, and have never had, an extra-territorial or even regional agenda. Instead, they once were people the world could do business without fear of violence. As the veteran journalist and author Eric Margolis has written, the now demonized Mullah Omar and his militia were once fairly hospitable folks who received hefty financial aid from the US just a few months before 9/11 and with whom Chevron and Unocal were keen to negotiate oil and gas pipeline deals.[277] Why then have the US policymakers continued to *maintain* Taliban as a threat to the United States. Here is another guess that may be disconcerting to some, "Too many in the United States cannot— or do not want to—distinguish between al Qaeda and the Taliban because an enemy, any

---

[272] Goodson, Afghanistan's Endless War, 109.

[273] Friedman, "Strategic Divergence."

[274] Leon Panetta, "There May Be Fewer Than 50 Al Qaeda Fighters In Afghanistan," AP/Huffington Post, June 27, 2010, http://www.huffingtonpost.com/2010/06/27/leon-panetta-there-may-be_n_627012.html (accessed October 22, 2010).

[275] George Friedman, "Strategic Divergence."

[276] Jihadism in 2009: The Trends Continue, *Stratfor*, January 7, 2009, http://www.stratfor.com/weekly/20090107_jihadism_2009_trends_continue (accessed October 10, 2010).

[277] Eric Margolis, "Let's Speak the Truth About Afghanistan," *The Huffington Post*, July 30, 2008, http://www.huffingtonpost.com/eric-margolis/lets-speak-the-truth-abou_b_115591.html (accessed October 25, 2010).

enemy, is good for business and provides fodder for Washington advisory organizations who thrive on strategic challenges and joint, interagency operations for their continued relevance and existence."[278]

A National Army *sans* a Nation

Despite their best efforts, the British could not rely on Shah Shuja's forces and had to garrison across Afghanistan to establish the writ of the state. While retreating from Kabul, no one was there to guard the flank of the once mighty Army of the Indus as the tribesmen were tearing away at it piece by piece.

The Soviet experience was no different. Soviets converted their agreement on military assistance to Afghanistan into "a carte blanche to modernize Afghanistan's armed forces."[279] However, as the unjustness of the Soviet agenda in Afghanistan dawned on the soldiers of the Afghan National Army, minor mutinies became frequent, and sometimes complete Afghan units, or sub-units deserted with their arms to Resistance groups.[280] Soviet attempts at ideological indoctrination also failed as many of their potential recruits escaped to join the streams of refugees heading for Pakistan.[281]

The story of the US-NATO efforts to stand up an Afghan National Army has had no better results. A top US army general told the US Army Times, "Extremely high illiteracy and desertion rates among Afghan army and police recruits have become the top challenges to standing up reliable Afghan security forces."[282] Many analysts term President Obama's July 2011 drawdown timeline as unrealistic mainly because, after years of supposedly determined effort, the "Afghanistan's security forces are not up to the task of taking charge of the war-torn country."[283] William Caldwell, the General supervising

---

[278] Warner, "Context and What's Next."
[279] Goodson, *Afghanistan's Endless War*, 52.
[280] O'Ballance, *Afghan Wars*, 99.
[281] Ibid., 99.
[282] Andrew Tilghman, "Illiteracy, desertion slow Afghan training," *ArmyTimes*, Tuesday Aug 24, 2010, http://www.armytimes.com/news/2010/08/military-afghan-army-illiteracy-082310w/ (accessed August 31, 2010,)
[283] Talbi, "US looks to Iraq strategy."

training of Afghan Army and Police has recently admitted, "We're training 3 Afghans to get 1 soldier. Just to grow to 56,000, we're going to have to recruit and train and assign 141,000 police and soldiers."[284]

According to a report in late 2009 one out of every four or five men in the security forces quit each year, meaning that tens of thousands must be recruited just to maintain the status quo.[285] The report further said that the number of Afghan battalions able to fight independently actually declined in the preceding six months.[286] Frustrated with the lack of progress in this area, US General David Petraeus has even pressed for raising what are now called Local Police Forces -- armed men paid by the government to defend their villages.[287] The Afghan President Karzai has however opposed this so-called village militia plan fearing such outfits could ruin his country further.[288]

The real problem is deeper than most policymakers appreciate. Volney Warner got to the heart of it when he wrote, "you need a nation to have a national army, and this nation only existed in Kabul and immediate environs."[289] With thugs and dummies running the government, with non-resident crooks and their cronies heading most of the state institutions, with the largest ethnic group largely alienated, with the populace generally feeling occupied, and with most of the rural country in the hands of resistance fighters, even the best of efforts are not likely to succeed in building dependable law enforcement agencies for Afghanistan.

The Surges and Numbers: It's Political Science not Mathematics

It is the foremost responsibility of the rulers and policymakers to ensure that their Generals have the right forces and the right policy before they lead young men and women into the war. The British initial numbers may have been adequate for the mission, but as the resistance intensified, the fighting

---

[284] "We are training three Afghans to get 1 Soldier," *CNN*, August 23, 2010, http://afghanistan.blogs.cnn.com/2010/08/23/general-were-training-3-afghans-to-get-1-soldier/ (accessed September 23, 2010).
[285] Thom Shanker and John H. Cushman Jr, "Reviews Raise Doubt on Training of Afghan Forces," *The New York Times*, November 5, 2009, http://www.nytimes.com/2009/11/06/world/asia/06training.html?_r=1 (accessed October 26, 2010).
[286] Ibid.
[287] Talbi, "US looks to Iraq strategy."
[288] Ibid.
[289] Warner, "Context and What's Next."

strength of the British Army of Indus actually declined. Much needed and promised reinforcements never arrived.

The strength of the Limited Contingent of the Soviet Forces in Afghanistan by the end of 1983, hovered around 110,000.[290] Unlike the US's incremental approach in the ongoing war, the Soviets entered Afghanistan "in a seemingly surgical fashion and with overwhelming force."[291] However, much like the fate of their predecessor, "the immense and stark territory of Afghanistan swallowed the invaders up."[292] The Soviets eventually discovered that no amount of military force was large enough to govern a country that was "less a nation than an agglomeration of some 25,000 village-states, each of which is largely self-governing and self-sufficient."[293]

From the modest numbers of early days, the Coalition boots on the ground in Afghanistan have now surged past 100,000. However, the real challenges seem to defy military numbers. While most US policy planners tend to see the surge as a game of numbers, on the ground it means better politics. Simon and Stevenson believe that a number-based surge formula was likely to "empower warlords, increase factionalism, and ultimately make Afghanistan harder to sustain as a functioning unitary state."[294] Empirical evidence supports this apparently extreme view. Despite repeated and significant increases in numbers of the US-NATO forces as well as newly re-created Afghan Army and Police, the security incidents have increased more than tenfold since 2004.[295]

What Afghanistan needs is a surge of hope, freedom, good governance, economic opportunity, and an equitable distribution of power. If the US-led coalition delivers even a fraction of that, Afghans would remember them as their friends and benefactors. In the words of David Miliband, UK's former

---

[290] O'Ballance, *Afghan Wars*, 121.
[291] Lester W. Grau, ed., *The Bear Went Over the Mountain: Soviet Combat Tactics in Afghanistan* (Washington, DC: National University Press), xi.
[292] Ibid.
[293] Anthony Arnold, *Afghanistan: The Soviet Invasion in Perspective* (India: Arnold-Heinemann Publishers, 1987), 97.
[294] Simon and Stevenson, "Afghanistan," 51.
[295] Collins, "The Path to Victory"

Foreign Secretary, "Military and civilian resources (both coalition's and Afghan) have to be aligned behind a clear political strategy."[296] Noted columnist Conn Hallinan also thinks this war "can only be solved by sitting all the parties down and working out a political settlement."[297]

---

[296] "Afghanistan 'not war without end'," *BBC News*, November 17, 2009, http://news.bbc.co.uk/2/hi/8364070.stm (accessed October 26, 2010).
[297] Conn Hallinan, "Why the Afghan Surge Will Fail," November 16, 2009, http://www.huffingtonpost.com/conn-hallinan/why-the-afghan-surge-will_b_355571.html (accessed October 26, 2010).

Recommendations

This monograph has attempted to indicate what *should not* have been done in Afghanistan. It seems fitting to end it on identification of some areas that deserve the attention of both the policymakers and the operational planners.

For the Strategist

Due to its current stage of socio-economic development and centuries of existence as a loose confederation of independent villages and tribes, it is a mistake for policymakers to apply the western idea of a state to Afghanistan. Throughout most of its history, Afghanistan has been a collection of fiercely independent people and repeated attempts to force a transition into a centrally governed state have proved still-borne. The unique paradox of this country is that it has always found its unity in division and its identity in diversity. Any effort to reverse that historical trend or reality will be a misdirected investment of blood and money. While the Afghans deserve a civilized and stable future, the US-NATO policymakers must learn to reconcile their desires with Afghanistan's reality.

While it is admirable that the ISAF Counterinsurgency Directive emphasizes protection of the civilians, the same may not be completely achievable in the short run. Policymakers need to understand that Afghans' top-most concern is poverty rather than protection. The history proves that Afghans are fully capable of protecting themselves. Moreover, the Coalition cannot hope to achieve the troop level required to extend physical protection to the populace across Afghanistan. The US-NATO Coalition should therefore avoid making promises it does not need to make or that it cannot keep, and promises mean a lot in Afghanistan. [298]

Throughout its troubled history, Afghanistan has seldom experienced *total* peace. Due to myriad factors like poverty, illiteracy, frequent foreign raids, and a tradition of *badal* (revenge), local and general conflict has been persistent. At least in the short run, therefore, no amount of money, time, or effort can

---

[298] Mehar Omar Khan, "Don't Try to Arrest the Sea: An Alternative Approach for Afghanistan," *Small Wars Journal*, October 2, 2009, http://smallwarsjournal.com/blog/2009/10/an-alternative-approach-for-af/%20[] (accessed October 25, 2009)

reverse this tragic historical reality. Policymakers must understand that bringing peace to this troubled nation will demand sincere national leadership and international commitment for next several decades.

Afghanistan has always been a *Pashtun* country. For centuries now, Afghanistan has been ruled by *Pashtuns*. Other ethnic groups like Uzbeks, Tajiks, and Hazaras have always existed on the fringe of the political mainstream. Therefore, while a participative and all-inclusive democratic polity may be a noble objective, it has but slim chances of becoming a reality anytime soon. Any attempt to deprive *Pashtuns* of their traditional right to the throne of Kabul, regardless of the questionable legitimacy of their claim, will invoke a violent reaction. In this backdrop, policymakers must understand that the ongoing Taliban (read *Pashtun*) insurgency is a quest of Afghanistan's traditional rulers for control a country they have always considered *theirs*.

For the Operational Artist

In line with the last policy recommendation above, operational planners should not treat *Pashtuns* at par with other groups. As of now, *Pashtuns* must be extended the treatment due to former, and long-time, rulers of Afghanistan. Within *Pashtuns*, planners must learn to appreciate the difference between the *qalang* values of the town and the *nang* traditional code of *Pashtunwali*. *Qalang* values are like those of rug merchants: they sit on the streets, they put a price tag on their thing, they bargain without attempting to hide the greed in their eyes, and they ultimately sell their thing to the highest bidder. The *nang* traditions of the mountains are different. They have little to sell and they do not know how to bargain. They will give their life to a friend and easily fight to death against someone they consider their enemy. Their price is respect, dignity, empathy, and understanding.

The majority of Afghans lives in villages. The legitimate authority in these units of Afghan population resides with the tribal elder *as well as* the local religious dynasty. Planners must learn to engage both. In the recent decades, because of the pervasiveness of the idea of Jihad against the Soviets, the religious clerics have come up as a challenge to the traditional tribal leadership. In this tug of war, the clergy has tried to portray, with a degree of success, the tribal elder or Malik as a vestige of the past injustices and as an institution that is neither representative of nor loyal to the sentiment of the man on the street. It is therefore a mistake to try to sideline the clergy and work entirely through the tribal chiefs.

Human beings in any corner of the world richly deserve a democratic choice, women's rights, and other basic freedoms. However, different societies are at different stages of their socio-economic development. Places like Afghanistan, ravaged by ceaseless conflict for last three decades, deserve an extraordinary level of understanding in these regards. A lot of what is seen on the streets of Kabul or Kandahar and out in the villages and valleys, is an effect or outcome of the traumatic years of war. Afghans as a society have lost, literally lost, more than four decades of natural evolution and growth. Within these four decades, the hooves of violence have beaten the tracks of tradition further down. Therefore, the best course of action for friends of Afghanistan would be to start where the Afghans actually *are* and not where the rest of the world stands.

A good strategy for Afghanistan would be one that, first and foremost, sets a very clear definition of the enemy. It is not just a question of who's the enemy. It is about time to also ask 'why'. Regardless of the myriad interpretations and viewpoints, the *Pashtuns* find the present dispensation in Kabul as unfavorable. They are the largest ethnic group, the traditional rulers of Afghanistan, and a host of organizations including Taliban represents their aspirations. More importantly however, planners need to acknowledge that *Pashtun* resistance will continue even if there were no such thing as Taliban. It is therefore time to de-hyphenate *Pashtuns* / Taliban from al Qaeda, and be heard and seen doing so. If the United States wants to be remembered as a friend of Afghanistan, it must get on the right side of the *Pashtuns*. They are a bad enemy and great friends. The single step of declaring al Qaeda alone to be the enemy of the United States will open up a range of options for the US-NATO strategy including an exit.

The Coalition's exit from Afghanistan also depends on the ability of the Afghan National Army and Police to take over responsibilities for the tasks currently being undertaken by NATO soldiers. With the largest ethnic group largely alienated, the project of recruiting and training Afghan national forces is not likely to take off. Such forces will have a long-term and sustained capacity only if the *Pashtuns* participate wholeheartedly. With their loyalties divided and the imminent possibility of Taliban's rise at the cost of the fledgling setup in Kabul, no able bodied *Pashtun* will wholeheartedly join or stay in the federal law enforcement agencies.

Lastly, governance has proven to be the single greatest vulnerability of the Coalition. The present administration in Kabul is not only corrupt; it is also inefficient, incompetent, and divided. Dominated by the warlords and thugs from the former Northern Alliance, the present government is a marriage of convenience between persons who hate each other and who will stay together only as long as the Coalition stays with all its money and military might. Sure, it is an elected government but it has been elected by people who are mostly illiterate and a majority of whom does not have a free choice. This house of cards is sure to fall apart soon after the departure of the Coalition troops or as soon as the Coalition money begins to dry up. For the sake of all those who have laid their lives and lost their limbs during the last ten years, the Coalition needs to start working on a broad-based, all-inclusive, and efficient government.

BIBLIOGRAPHY

Books

Aghajanian, Alfred, ed. *Afghanistan: Past and Present.* Los Angeles, CA: IndoEuropean Publishing.com, 2007.

Ahmed, Akbar S. *Journey into America: The Challenge of Islam.* Washington, DC: Brookings Institution Press, 2010.

Amstutz, J. Bruce. *Afghanistan: The First Five Years of Soviet Occupation.* Washington DC: National Defense University Press, 1986.

Chisholm, Hugh. *Encyclopedia Britannica* (Eleventh Edition, Published 1910-11), Library of Fogg Museum of Art, Harvard University.

Churchill, Sir Winston S., *The Story of the Malakand Field Force.* London: Longman, Green, and Co., 1901.

Clark, Jeffrey J. *Advice & Support: The Final Years 1965-1973.* Washington, DC: U.S. Army Center of Military History, 1988.

Cordesman, Anthony H. and Wagner, Abraham R. *The Lessons of Modern War Vol III: The Afghan and Falklands Conflicts.* Mansell Publishing Limited: London, 1990.

Entezar, Ehsan M. *Afhanistan 101: Understanding Afghan Culture.* USA: Xlibris Corporation, 2007.

Giustozzi, Antonio. *Koran, Kalashnikov,and Laptop: The Neo-Taliban Insurgency in Afghanistan.* New York: Columbia University Press, 2008.

Gohari, M.J. *The Taliban Ascent to Power.* Karachi: Oxford University Press, 2001.

Goodson, Larry P. *Afghanistan's Endless War: State Failure, Regional Politics and the Rise of Taliban.*Seattle: University of Washington Press, 2001.

Grau, Lester W. and Gress, Michael A. *The Soviet Afghan War: How a Super Power Fought and Lost / The Russian General Staff.* Lawrence: University Press of Kansas, 2002.

Grau, Lester W. *The Bear Went Over the Mountain: Soviet Combat Tactics in Afghanistan.* Washington, DC: National University Press.

Griffin, Michael. *Reaping the Whirlwind: The Taliban Movement in Afghanistan.* Sterling, Virginia: Pluto Press, 2001.

Griffin, Micheael. *Reaping the Whirlwind: The Taliban Movement in Afghanistan.* Sterling, VA: Pluto Press, 2001.

Gunderson, Corey. *Afghanistan's Struggles.* Edina, Minnesota: ABDO and Daughters, 2004.

Gupta, L. *Psychosocial Assessment of Children Exposed to War Related Violence in Kabul.* New York: Unicef, 1997.

Hamilton, Angus. *Afghanistan.* London: William Heinemann, 1906.

Hammond, Thomas Taylor. *Red flag over Afghanistan: The Communist coup, the Soviet invasion, and the consequences.* Boulder, Colo: Westview Press, 1984.

Haqqani, Hussain. *Pakistan: Between Mosque and Military.* Washington, DC: Carnegie Endowment for International Peace, 2005.

Hauner, Milan. *The Soviet war in Afghanistan: Patterns of Russian Imperialism.* Lanham, Md: University Press of America, 1991.

Holy Bible

Isby, David C. *War in a Distant Country: Afghanistan Invasion and Resistance.* London: Arms and Armour Pess, 1989.

Johnson, Chris and Leslie, Jolyol. *Afghanistan: The Mirage of Peace.* London: Zed Books Ltd, 2004.

Jones, Seth G., *In the Graveyard of Empires: America's War in Afghanistan.* New York: W.W. Norton and Company Inc., 2010.

Kellner, Douglas. *From 9/11 to Terror War: The Dangers of the Bush Legacy.* Lanham, Maryland: Rowman & Littlefield Publishers, Inc., 2003.

Kilcullen, David. *The Accidental Guerrilla: Fighting a Small War in the Midst of a Big One.* London: Hurst & Company.

Kipling, Joseph Rudyard. *The Works of Rudyard Kipling.* The Forgotton Books, 2008.

Kipling, Rudyard. *The Writings in Prose and Verse of Rudyard Kipling.* New York: Charles Scribner's Sons, 1899.

Loyn, David. *In Afghanistan: Two Hundred Years of British, Russian and American Occupation.* New York: Pelgrave MacMillan, 2009.

Maley, William. *The Afghanistan Wars.* New York: Pelgrave Mac Millan, 2002.

Neustadt, Richard E. and May, Earnest R. *Thinking in Time: The Uses of History for Decision Makers.* New York: The Free Press, 1988.

Norris, J.A. *The First Afghan War 1838-1842.* Cambridge: University Press, 1967.

O'Ballance, Edgar. *Afghan Wars: Battles in a Hostile Land.* UK: Brassey's, 2002.

Pigott, Peter. *Canada in Afghanistan: The War So Far.* Toronto: Dundurn Press, 2007.

Roberts, Jeffery J. *The Origins of Conflict in Afghanistan.* Westport, CT: Praeger Publishers, 2003.
Robson, Brian. *Crisis on the Frontier: The Third Afghan War and the Campaign in Waziristan 1919-1920.* Staplehurst, Kent: Spellmount Limited, 2004.

Robson, Brian. *Crisis on the Frontier: The Third Afghan War and the Campaign in Waziristan 1919-20.* Gloucestershire: Spellmount, 2007.

Rogers,Tom. *The Soviet Withdrawal from Afghanistan: Analysis and Chronology.* Westport, Connecticut: Greenwood Press, 1992.

Rubin, Barnett R. *The Fragmentation of Afghanistan.* Yale University Press, 2002.

Spector, Ronald. *Advice and Support: The Early Years, 1941-1960.* University Press of the Pacific, 2005.

Tanner, Stephen. *Afghanistan: A Military History from Alexander the Great to the War Against the Taliban.* Da Capo Press, 2002.

Thompson, Sir Robert G.K. *Defeating Communist Insurgency: The Lessons of Malaya and Vietnam.* New York: Praeger.

Vogelsang,William. *The Afghans.* Oxford, UK: Blackwell Publishers Ltd, 2002.

Vogelsang,William. *The Afghans.* Oxford, UK: Blackwell Publishers Ltd, 2002.

Others Sources

Amanpour, Christiane. "Tyranny of the Taliban." *Time*, June 24, 2001. Accessed October 5, 2010. http://www.time.com/time/magazine/article/0,9171,1101971013-136677,00.html

Baker, Aryn. "Afghan Women and the Return of the Taliban." *Time*, July 29, 2010. Accessed August 24, 2010. http://www.time.com/time/world/article/0,8599,2007238,00.html#ixzz0xXWOtjMb

Baker, Aryn. "Talking with the Taliban: Easier Said Than Done." Time Magazine, November 30, 2009. Accessed October 25, 2010. http://www.time.com/time/magazine/article/0,9171,1940679,00.html

Barfield, Thomas. "Problems of Establishing Legitimacy in Afghanistan." *Iranian Studies* 37, 2004.

Baumann, Robert F. "Compound War Case Study: The Soviets in Afghanistan," *GlobalSecurity.org.* Accessed 23 Sep, 2010. http://www.globalsecurity.org/military/library/report/2001/soviet-afghan_compound-warfare.htm

Burke, Jason. "Bin Laden ready to leave hideout," *Guardian UK*, October 31, 1999. Accessed September 16, 2010. http://www.guardian.co.uk/world/1999/oct/31/afghanistan

Burke, Jason. "Waiting for a last battle with the Taliban." *The Guardian*, June 27, 1999. Accessed October 27, 2010. http://www.guardian.co.uk/world/1999/jun/27/afghanistan

Bush, George W., President of the United States of America. Address to a Joint Session of Congress and the American People at the United States Capitol Washington, D.C., September 20, 2010. Accessed October 19, 2010. http://georgewbush-whitehouse.archives.gov/news/releases/2001/09/20010920-8.html

Chivers, C.J. "General Faces Unease Among His Own Troops, Too." *The New York Times*, June 22, 2010. Accessed August 31, 2010. http://www.nytimes.com/2010/06/23/world/asia/23troops.html

Christia, Fotini and Semple, Michael. 'Flipping the Taliban.' *Foreign Affairs*, 88-4, July–August 2009. http://www.foreignaffairs.com/articles/65151/fotini-christia-and-michael-semple/flipping-the-taliban

CIA. "Afghanistan: The World Fact Book." Accessed 20 Sep 10. https://www.cia.gov/library/publications/the-world-factbook/geos/af.html

CNN. "We are training three Afghans to get 1 Soldier." August 23, 2010. Accessed September 23, 2010. http://afghanistan.blogs.cnn.com/2010/08/23/general-were-training-3-afghans-to-get-1-soldier/

CNN. "Who are the Taliban of Afghanistan." October 05, 1996. Accessed on October 5, 2010. http://articles.cnn.com/1996-10-05/world/9610_05_taleban_1_taliban-islamic-militia-kabul-islamic-afghanistan?_s=PM:WORLD

Cohen, Eliot A. "Obama's COIN toss," *The Washington Post*, December 6, 2009. Accessed October 22, 2010. http://www.washingtonpost.com/wp-dyn/content/article/2009/12/04/AR2009120402602.html

Coll, Steve. "Gorbachev Was Right." *The New Yorker,* September 29, 2009. Accessed October 22, 2010. http://www.newyorker.com/online/blogs/stevecoll/2009/09/gorbachev-was-right.html

Collins, Joseph J. "Afghanistan: The Path to Victory," *JFQ 54* (2009).

Collins, Joseph J. "Afghanistan: The Path to Victory," *JFQ 54* (2009).

Diehl, Jackson. "Obama's Karzai problem." *The Washington Post*, February 24, 2010. Accessed October 22, 2010. http://voices.washingtonpost.com/postpartisan/2010/02/karzai.html

Dobbins, James. "Counterinsurgency in Afghanistan - Testimony presented before the House Oversight and Government Reform Committee, Subcommittee on National Security and Foreign Affairs on March 26, 2009, CT-323 March 2009. *RAND Corporation.* Accessed October 20, 2010, http://www.rand.org/pubs/testimonies/CT323/

Dobbs, Michael. "The Afghan Archive: Secret Memos Trace Kremlin's March to War." *The Washington Post*, 15 November 1992. Accessed on October 21, 2010. http://www.encyclopedia.com/The+Washington+Post/publications.aspx?date=19921115&pageNumber=1

Dodd, Mark. "AFP faces struggles to train Afghans." *The Australian*, October 21, 2010. Accessed October 22, 2010. http://www.theaustralian.com.au/national-affairs/defence/afp-faces-struggles-to-train-afghans/story-e6frg8yo-1225941412641

Friedman, George. "Now for the Hard Part: From Iraq to Afghanistan." *Stratfor*, July 15, 2008. Accessed September 20, 2010. http://www.stratfor.com/weekly/now_hard_part_iraq_afghanistan

Friedman, George. "Strategic Divergence: The War Against the Taliban and the War Against Al Qaeda." *Stratfor Global Intelligence*, January 26, 2009. Accessed May 25, 2010. http://www.stratfor.com/weekly/20090126_strategic_divergence_war_against_taliban_and_war_against_al_qaeda

Friedman, George. "Strategic Divergence: The War Against the Taliban and the War Against Al Qaeda." *Stratfor*, January 26, 2009. Accessed October 20, 2010. http://www.stratfor.com/weekly/20090126_strategic_divergence_war_against_taliban_and_war_against_al_qaeda

Garcia, J. Malcolm. *"Most Dangerous, Most Unmerciful,"* VQR (Spring 2010). Accessed October 1, 2010. http://www.vqronline.org/articles/2010/spring/garcia-most-dangerous/

Gates, Robert M. "A Balanced Strategy: Reprogramming the Pentagon for a New Age." *Foreign Affairs* 88, no. 1 (January-February 2009). http://web.ebscohost.com/ehost/detail?vid=7&hid=106&sid=028e9f71-84b8-4e24-971d-c4191b964831%40sessionmgr104&bdata=JnNpdGU9ZWhvc3QtbGl2ZQ%3d%3d#db=aph&AN=35634218 .

Ghosh, Bobby. "Afghan Mission Creep: Back to Nation-Building," *Time*, August 19, 2009. Accessed September 23, 2010. http://www.time.com/time/nation/article/0,8599,1917232,00.html#ixzz10NOf2tM9

Gvosdev, Nikolas K. "The Soviet Victory that Never Was." *Foreign Affairs*, December 10, 2010. Accessed October 22, 2010. http://www.foreignaffairs.com/articles/65713/nikolas-k-gvosdev/the-soviet-victory-that-never-was?page=2

Hallinan, Conn. "Why the Afghan Surge Will Fail," *The Huffington Post,* November 16, 2009. Accessed October 26, 2010. http://www.huffingtonpost.com/conn-hallinan/why-the-afghan-surge-will_b_355571.html

Hatch Dupree, Nancy. Afghanistan through the eyes of Pakistani cartoonists. Baba, 1994.

Hersh, Seymour M. "The Other War: Why Bush's Afghanistan problem won't go away." *The New Yorker*, April 12, 2004. Accessed October 19, 2010. http://www.newyorker.com/archive/2004/04/12/040412fa_fact http://www.upi.com/Top_News/Special/2010/09/28/Petraeus-backs-talks-with-Taliban/UPI-16661285696545/

Johnson, Thomas H. and Mason, M. Chris. "Refighting the Last War: Afghanistan and the Vietnam Template," *Military Review*, November-December 2009.

Johnson, Thomas H. and Mason, M. Chris. "Refighting the Last War: Afghanistan and the Vietnam Template." *Military Review*, November-December 2009.

Johnson, Thomas H. and Mason, M. Chris. "Understanding the Taliban and Insurgency in Afghanistan." *Orbis* 51 (Winter 2007). Accessed online on September 23, 2010. http://www.fpri.org/orbis/5101/

Johnston, David. "Charlie Wilson's War': Arming the Mujahedeen." *The New York Times*, May 25, 2003. Accessed on October 5, 2010. http://www.grailwerk.com/docs/nytimes10.htm

Khan, Mehar Omar. "Don't try to arrest the sea: An alternative approach for Afghanistan." *Small Wars Journal*, October 2, 2009. Accessed October 25, 2009. http://smallwarsjournal.com/blog/2009/10/an-alternative-approach-for-af/

Koelbl, Susanne. "The Taliban Kills more Civilians than NATO." *Spiegel International*, September 24, 2007. Accessed October 5, 2010. http://www.spiegel.de/international/world/0,1518,508021,00.html

Kulakov, Oleg. "Lessons learned from the Soviet Intervention in Afghanistan: Implications for Russian Defense Reform." *NATO Defense College, Research Paper No. 26* (March 2006)

Lamb, Christopher J. and Cinnamond, Martin. "Unified Effort: Key to Special Operations and Irregular Warfare in Afghanistan." *Joint Forces Quarterly* 56 (2010).

Lasseter, Tom. "Afghanistan war: Russian vets look back on their experience." The Christian Science Monitor, December 22, 2009. Accessed 23 Sep 2010. http://www.csmonitor.com/World/2009/1222/Afghanistan-war-Russian-vets-look-back-on-their-experience

Lev, Michael A. "Taliban maintains refusal to turn over bin Laden." *Los Angeles Times*, October 3, 2001. Accessed on October 5, 2010. http://www.latimes.com/sns-worldtrade-taliban-chi,0,1586746.story

Margolis, Eric. "Let's Speak the Truth About Afghanistan," *The Huffington Post*, July 30, 2008. Accessed October 25, 2010. http://www.huffingtonpost.com/eric-margolis/lets-speak-the-truth-abou_b_115591.html

Nagle, John A. "A Better War in Afghanistan." *JFQ,* Issue 56, 1st quarter [2010].

New Zealand Herald, October 9, 2010. "The other Karzai." Accessed October 22, 2010. http://www.nzherald.co.nz/world/news/article.cfm?c_id=2&objectid=10679291

North, Andrew. "Soviet lessons from Afghanistan." *BBC News*, 18 November 2009. Accessed October 22, 2010. http://news.bbc.co.uk/2/hi/south_asia/8365187.stm

North, Andrew. "Soviet lessons from Afghanistan." *BBC News*, November 18, 2009. Accessed October 22, 2010. http://news.bbc.co.uk/2/hi/south_asia/8365187.stm

O'Hanlon, Michael. "Toward Reconciliation in Afghanistan." *The Washington Quarterly* 32:2, April 2009. Accessed October 15, 2010. http://www.twq.com/09april/docs/09apr_OHanlon.pdf

Palu, Louie. "Total War," *VQR* [spring 2010]

Panetta, Leon. "There May Be Fewer Than 50 Al Qaeda Fighters In Afghanistan." *AP/Huffington Post*, June 27, 2010. Accessed October 22, 2010. http://www.huffingtonpost.com/2010/06/27/leon-panetta-there-may-be_n_627012.html

Parry, Robert. "How Bush Botched the Afghan War?" *Baltimore Chronicle and Sentinel*, 27 July 2010. Accessed October 22, 2010. http://baltimorechronicle.com/2010/072710Parry.shtml

Petraeus, General David H. Commander, COMISAF's Counterinsurgency Guidance, 1 August 2010. Available online at http://www.isaf.nato.int/from-the-commander/from-the-commander/comisaf-s-counterinsurgency-guidance.html

Ralph, Peters, "Trapping Ourselves in Afghanistan and Losing Focus on the Essential Mission," *JFQ* 54 (2009)

Reeves, William. "Obituary: Dr Najibullah." The Independent (UK), September 28, 1996. Accessed on October 5, 2010. http://www.independent.co.uk/news/obituaries/obituary-dr-najibullah-1365378.html

Ricks, Thomas E. "The COINdinistas." *Foreign Policy*, December 1, 2009. Accessed October 22, 2010. http://www.foreignpolicy.com/articles/2009/11/30/the_coindinistas

Ringsmose, Jens and Thruelsen, Peter Dahl. "NATO´s counterinsurgency campaign in Afghanistan: Are classical doctrines suitable for alliances?," *UNISCI Discussion Papers,* (January 2010).

Rubin, Alissa J. "Karzai's Words Leave Few Choices for the West." *The New York Times*, April 4, 2010. Accessed October 22, 2010. http://www.nytimes.com/2010/04/05/world/asia/05karzai.html

Savranskaya, Svetlana ed. "The Soviet Experience in Afghanistan: Russian Documents and Memoirs (The September 11th Sourcebooks, Volume-II), October 9, 2001." *The National Security Archive.* Accessed September 20, 2010. http://www.gwu.edu/~nsarchiv/NSAEBB/NSAEBB57/soviet.html

Shalizi, Hamid. "Afghans pay off Taliban with 'American money." *Reuters*, October 13, 2010. Accessed October 22, 2010. http://www.msnbc.msn.com/id/39646568/ns/world_news-south_and_central_asia/

Shanker, Tom. and Cushman Jr., John H. "Reviews Raise Doubt on Training of Afghan Forces." *The New York Times*, November 5, 2009. Accessed October 26, 2010. http://www.nytimes.com/2009/11/06/world/asia/06training.html?_r=1

Simon, Steven and Stevenson, Jonathan. "Afghanistan: How Much is Enough?", *Survival,* 51: 5.

Stolberg, Sheryl Gay. "Obama Defends Strategy in Afghanistan." *The New York Times*, August 17, 2009. Accessed October 22, 2010. http://www.nytimes.com/2009/08/18/us/politics/18vets.html

Stratfor, January 7, 2009. "Jihadism in 2009: The Trends Continue." Accessed October 10, 2010. http://www.stratfor.com/weekly/20090107_jihadism_2009_trends_continue

Talbi, Karim. "US looks to Iraq strategy for Afghanistan." *The China Post*, August 24, 2010. Accessed October 20, 2010. http://www.chinapost.com.tw/commentary/afp/2010/08/24/269865/US-looks.htm

Taubman, Philip. "Soviet Lists Afghan War Toll: 13,310 Dead, 35,478 Wounded." *The New York Times*, May 26, 1988. Accessed October 5, 2010. http://www.nytimes.com/1988/05/26/world/soviet-lists-afghan-war-toll-13310-dead-35478-wounded.html

Taubman, Philip. "Soviet Lists Afghan War Toll: 13,310 Dead, 35,478 Wounded." *The New York Times*, May 26, 1988. Accessed October 25, 2010. http://www.nytimes.com/1988/05/26/world/soviet-lists-afghan-war-toll-13310-dead-35478-wounded.html

Taylor Jr., William B. and Their, J. Alexander. "The Road to Successful Transition in Afghanistan: From Here to the December 2010 Review." *United States Institute of Peace*, PeaceBrief No.30, May 12, 2010. Accessed October 15, 2010. http://www.usip.org/node/1726/resources-tools

Telegraph, UK. "Taliban control half of Afghanistan, says report." November 22, 2007. Accessed October 22, 2010. http://www.telegraph.co.uk/news/worldnews/1570232/Taliban-control-half-of-Afghanistan-says-report.html

The New York Times. "Soviet General Talks of Failure in Afghanistan." January 23, 1989. Accessed 23 September, 2010. http://www.nytimes.com/1989/01/23/world/soviet-general-talks-of-failure-in-afghanistan.html

The Washington Post. "Editorial: Bob Woodward's book portrays a great divide over Afghanistan." September 29, 2010. Accessed October 22, 2010. http://www.washingtonpost.com/wp-dyn/content/article/2010/09/28/AR2010092805200.html

The World Bank. "Afghanistan Country Overview." Accessed September 15, 2010. http://www.worldbank.org.af/WBSITE/EXTERNAL/COUNTRIES/SOUTHASIAEXT/AFGHANISTANEXTN/0,,contentMDK:20154015~menuPK:305992~pagePK:141137~piPK:141127~theSitePK:305985,00.html

Tilghman, Andrew. "Illiteracy, desertion slow Afghan training." *ArmyTimes*, Tuesday Aug 24, 2010. Accessed August 31, 2010. http://www.armytimes.com/news/2010/08/military-afghan-army-illiteracy-082310w/

Twining, Dan., "What is Obama's real 'Exit Strategy' for Afghanistan? And why it matters to India." *Foreign Policy*, December 3, 2009. Accessed October 22, 2010. http://shadow.foreignpolicy.com/posts/2009/12/03/what_is_obamas_real_exit_strategy_for_afghanistan_and_why_it_matters_to_india

Tyson, Ann Scott. "In Helmand, Caught between U.S., Taliban; 'Skittish' Afghans Wary of Both Sides." *The Washington Post*, August 15, 2009. Accessed October 20, 2010, http://www.washingtonpost.com/wp-dyn/content/article/2009/08/14/AR2009081403568.html

UNICEF. "Afghanistan." Accessed 20 Sep 10. http://www.unicef.org/infobycountry/afghanistan_statistics.html

UPI.com. "Petraeus backs talks with Taliban." September 28, 2010. Accessed October 22, 2010.

Warner, Volney F. "Context and What's Next." *Joint Forces Quarterly / issue 56, 1st quarter, 2010.*

Ingram Content Group UK Ltd.
Milton Keynes UK
UKHW030636170523
421890UK00008B/244